Workshop on Computing Semantics with Types, Frames and Related Structures (CSTFRS 2019)

Gothenburg, Sweden
24 May 2019

ISBN: 978-1-5108-8765-7

Printed from e-media with permission by:

Curran Associates, Inc.
57 Morehouse Lane
Red Hook, NY 12571

Printed by Curran Associates, Inc. (2019)

For permission requests, please contact the Association for Computational Linguistics at the address below.

Association for Computational Linguistics
209 N. Eighth Street
Stroudsburg, Pennsylvania 18360

Phone: 1-570-476-8006
Fax: 1-570-476-0860

acl@aclweb.org

Additional copies of this publication are available from:

Curran Associates, Inc.
57 Morehouse Lane
Red Hook, NY 12571 USA
Phone: 845-758-0400
Fax: 845-758-2633
Email: curran@proceedings.com
Web: www.proceedings.com

CSTFRS 2019

IWCS 2019 Workshop on Computing Semantics with Types, Frames and Related Structures

Proceedings of the Workshop

May 24, 2019
Gothenburg, Sweden

Introduction

The Workshop on Computing Semantics with Types, Frames and Related Structures, colocated with the 13th International Conference on Computational Semantics (IWCS 2019), is intended as a forum for people interested in structured representations of linguistic information, especially from a computational perspective.

Structured representations play a central role in the study of natural language semantics, especially in cognitively oriented approaches in the tradition of Fillmore, Jackendoff, and Langacker. Formal semantics in the Montague-tradition, on the other hand, is less concerned with the structure of representations but with logical expressions, truth conditions, and model-theoretic interpretations. In recent years, however, there has been a growing body of research which aims to integrate structured entities into formal semantic accounts. Important developments in this field are the uses of rich type systems and frame-based representations in lexical and compositional semantics. A key feature of these approaches is that semantic representations can themselves be used to compute semantic content and have yielded a way of combining compositional and lexical semantics by providing a single representational system for different modalities.

The topics of this workshop cover both foundational issues (e.g. developments in rich type theoretical semantics) and applications of theories that employ structured representations to specific linguistic phenomena.

We would like to thank the organizers of IWCS 2019 for hosting our workshop in Gothenburg.

Rainer Osswald
Christian Retoré
Peter Sutton

Program Chairs & Organization

Rainer Osswald, Heinrich Heine University Düsseldorf (Germany)
Christian Retoré, Université de Montpellier & LIRMM (France)
Peter Sutton, Heinrich Heine University Düsseldorf (Germany)

Program Committee

Daisuke Bekki, Ochanomizu University (Japan)
Ellen Breitholtz, University of Gothenburg (Sweden)
Stergios Chatzikyriakidis, University of Gothenburg (Sweden)
Robin Cooper, University of Gothenburg (Sweden)
Jonathan Ginzburg, Université Paris-Diderot (France)
Eleni Gregoromichelaki, Heinrich Heine University Düsseldorf (Germany)
Justyna Grudzińska, University of Warsaw (Poland)
Laura Kallmeyer, Heinrich Heine University Düsseldorf (Germany)
Zhaohui Luo, Royal Holloway – University of London (UK)
Bruno Mery, Université de Bordeaux (France)
Richard Moot, Université de Montpellier & LIRMM (France)
Reinhard Muskens, Tilburg University (The Netherlands)
Valeria de Paiva, Nuance Communications & University of Birmingham (UK)
Sylvain Pogodalla, INRIA Nancy – Grand Est, LORIA Lab (France)
James Pustejovsky, Brandeis University (USA)
Livy Real, Universidade de São Paulo (Brasil)
Marek Zawadowski, University of Warsaw (Poland)
Henk Zeevat, Heinrich Heine University Düsseldorf (Germany)

Table of Contents

Workshop Program

Friday, May 24, 2019

9:15–9:30 ***Opening Remarks***

9:30–10:00 *Underspecification and interpretive parallelism in Dependent Type Semantics*
Yusuke Kubota, Koji Mineshima, Robert Levine and Daisuke Bekki

10:00–10:30 ***Coffee***

10:30–11:00 *Translating a Fragment of Natural Deduction System for Natural Language into Modern Type Theory*
Ivo Pezlar

11:00–11:30 *Modeling the Induced Action Alternation and the Caused-Motion Construction with Tree Adjoining Grammar (TAG) and Semantic Frames*
Esther Seyffarth

11:30–12:00 *Complex event representation in a typed feature structure implementation of Role and Reference Grammar*
Erika Bellingham

12:00–13:30 ***Lunch***

13:30–14:00 *Computational Syntax-Semantics Interface with Type-Theory of Acyclic Recursion for Underspecified Semantics*
Roussanka Loukanova

14:00–14:30 *Modeling language constructs with compatibility intervals*
Pavlo Kapustin and Michael Kapustin

14:30–15:00 *ImageTTR: Grounding Type Theory with Records in Image Classification for Visual Question Answering*
Arild Matsson, Simon Dobnik and Staffan Larsson

15:00–15:30 *Enthymemetic Conditionals: Topoi as a guide for acceptability*
Eimear Maguire

15:30 ***Coffee***

Friday, May 24, 2019 (continued)

15:30–16:00 *General discussion and closing*

Underspecification and interpretive parallelism in Dependent Type Semantics

Yusuke Kubota
National Institute for
Japanese Language and Linguistics
kubota@ninjal.ac.jp

Koji Mineshima
Ochanomizu University
mineshima.koji@ocha.ac.jp

Robert Levine
Ohio State University
levine.1@osu.edu

Daisuke Bekki
Ochanomizu University
bekki@is.ocha.ac.jp

Abstract

The scope parallelism in the Geach sentence (*Every boy loves, and every girl detests, some saxophonist*) and the related parallel interpretation requirement in pronominal binding is a pervasive phenomenon found across different types of coordination and ellipsis phenomena. Previous accounts all resort to additional constraints of some sort that restrict the otherwise flexible syntax-semantics interface to avoid overgeneration. In this paper, we propose a novel approach to this long-standing problem. We show that, by taking a proof-theoretic perspective on natural language semantics and by viewing the ambiguity resolution for pronouns and indefinites as underspecification resolution that invokes extra proof search, a conceptually natural solution emerges for the problem of interpretive parallelism. The analysis is cast in Dependent Type Semantics, with Hybrid Type-Logical Categorial Grammar as the syntax-semantics interface backbone. For empirical illustration, we show how the proposed approach correctly accounts for the classical Geach paradigm and its pronominal variant.

1 Introduction: interpretive parallelism in coordination and ellipsis

One of the long-standing problems in the analysis of coordination and ellipsis is the strong parallelism requirement imposed on the interpretations of the 'shared' linguistic expression. For example, Geach (1972) famously noticed that, in the following type of examples involving right-node raising (RNR), the object indefinite that is shared in the two conjuncts can either scope below the subject quantifier in each conjunct or scope over the entire coordination, but that mixed scope readings, in which the object indefinite scopes above the subject quantifier in one conjunct but not in the other, are unavailable.

(1) Every boy loves, and every girl detests, some saxophonist. $(\forall > \exists \wedge \forall > \exists \,/\, \exists > \forall \wedge \exists > \forall)$

Jacobson (1999) notes that this interpretive parallelism extends to the pronominal variable binding in examples such as the following (on reading 2, John is a salient male individual in the discourse):

(2) Every Englishman admires, and every American loves, his mother.
reading 1: 'Every Englishman admires his own mother, and every American loves his own mother.'
reading 2: 'Every Englishman admires John's mother, and every American loves John's mother.'

In general, pronouns can either be free or bound by a quantifier. Thus, there are four logically possible interpretations for (2) (bound/free in first/second conjunct). And all these interpretations are indeed available in the non-RNR counterpart of (2) (*Every Englishman admires his mother and every American loves his mother*). However, only two of these readings are attested for (2), as indicated above.

The parallel interpretation requirement is not limited to coordination but extends to ellipsis phenomena. For example, Hirschbühler (1982) notes that VP ellipsis imposes parallelism requirement for the scope of the quantifier inside the 'elided' material, in a way essentially parallel to the RNR sentences:

Proceedings of the IWCS 2019 Workshop on Computing Semantics with Types, Frames and Related Structures, pages 1–9
Gothenburg, Sweden, May 24, 2019.

(3) An American flag was hanging in front of every window. A Canadian flag was, too.

Like the RNR example in (1), there are only the $\forall > \exists \wedge \forall > \exists$ and $\exists > \forall \wedge \exists > \forall$ parallel scope readings for this sentence. Mixed scope readings in which the universal scopes over the indefinite in the antecedent but not in the ellipsis site (or vice versa) are unavailable.

Just as the RNR parallelism for quantifier scope in (1) is mirrored in the anaphora case in (2), the scopal parallelism in the VP ellipsis data in (3) has an exact analogue in the anaphora example in (4).

(4) Every Englishman admires his mother, and every American does as well.

As in (2), the admiration relation holds either between every Englishman and every American male and his own respective mother or between every Englishman and every American male and the mother of some specific male individual in the antecedent context, with no mixed reading possible.

The parallelism patterns in (1) and (2) recur in the case of Stripping (see Puthawala (2018) for a recent formal analysis of Stripping, as well as a discussion of important properties of this construction).

(5) a. Every boy admires a saxophonist, and every girl too.
b. Every Englishman admires his mother, and every American as well.

These examples exhibit only the parallel interpretations (analogous to the relevant readings for the RNR and VP ellipsis examples given above) for the quantifier or pronoun contained in the elided material.

The interpretive parallelism in the data surveyed above has been noted by many authors (see, e.g., Jacobson 1999; Fox 2000; Asudeh and Crouch 2002; Steedman 2012), but no uniform analysis currently exists which treats the binding and quantifier cases in a principled manner and which covers both the coordination and ellipsis cases. The present paper attempts to make a first step in such a unified analysis by focusing on the binding and scope data in RNR (i.e. the Geach paradigm). The key claim of our proposal is that interpretive parallelism is a consequence of the underspecification involved in the interpretation of pronouns and indefinites (in this sense, it is similar in spirit to Steedman's (2012) approach).

All the examples above have one property in common: the shared material contains an expression (pronoun/quantifier) that exhibits interpretive variability. Our proposal in a nutshell is that interpretive parallelism falls out from the way underspecification resolution happens in sentences that have this property, due to interactions of the following conceptually natural assumptions:

(i) interpretive variability is resolved by underspecification resolution, formalized as type-checking
(ii) for 'shared' material, the syntax-semantics mapping requires the duplication of resource at *some* point in the mapping from the surface string to the final, fully resolved translation
(iii) the formal language for the underspecified semantic representation imposes a certain restriction on the way multiple copies of an (originally) underspecified term are interpreted

The third condition can be thought to arise from the requirement to keep the mechanism simple for ensuring proper identity of underspecified terms with respect to their interpretive possibilities.

We show below that these simple assumptions suffice to ensure the right range of interpretations to be assigned to the examples discussed above, by taking the case of RNR as an example. We formulate our analysis in Dependent Type Semantics (DTS; Bekki 2014; Bekki and Mineshima 2017), by proposing a novel treatment of indefinites involving underspecification. The proof-theoretic perspective of DTS provides a particularly natural setup to embody the assumptions outlined in (i)–(iii) above. For the sake of explicitness, we adopt Hybrid Type-Logical Categorial Grammar (Hybrid TLCG; Kubota and Levine 2012, 2015) for the syntax-semantics interface in spelling out the analyses of specific linguistic examples. The choice of Hybrid TLCG for syntax is not essential, but we believe that it helps illuminate the general nature of our solution, which is compatible with any suitably general theory of compositional semantics.

$$\frac{\begin{array}{c}[x:A]^i\\ \vdots\\ A:\mathtt{t}\quad B:\mathtt{t}\end{array}}{(x:A)\to B:\mathtt{t}}\,\Pi F,i \qquad \frac{\begin{array}{c}[x:A]^i\\ \vdots\\ A:\mathtt{t}\quad B:\mathtt{t}\end{array}}{(x:A)\times B:\mathtt{t}}\,\Sigma F,i \qquad \frac{\begin{array}{c}[x:A]^i\\ \vdots\\ m:B\end{array}}{\lambda x.m:(x:A)\to B}\,\Pi I,i \qquad \frac{m:A\quad n:B[m/x]}{(m,n):(x:A)\times B}\,\Sigma I$$

$$\frac{f:(x:A)\to B\quad a:A}{f(a):B[a/x]}\,\Pi E \qquad \frac{c:(x:A)\times B}{\pi_1(c):A}\,\Sigma E \qquad \frac{c:(x:A)\times B}{\pi_2(c):B[\pi_1(c)/x]}\,\Sigma E$$

Figure 1: Inference rules: formation rules (ΠF, ΣF), introduction rules (ΠI, ΣI), elimination rules (ΠE, ΣE)

2 Anaphora and scope via underspecification in DTS

Dependent Type Theory (Martin-Löf 1984) is an extension of simply typed λ-calculus. Dependent Type Semantics (DTS) is a proof-theoretic compositional dynamic semantics based on Dependent Type Theory. This framework allows us to use *types depending on terms* and to represent propositions (corresponding to semantic representations of sentences) as types. For instance, $\mathbf{run}(x)$ is a type depending on a term x. Under the Curry-Howard correspondence (*propositions-as-types* principle), the type $\mathbf{run}(x)$ can be regarded as the proposition that x runs. If a term u has this type, we write $u : \mathbf{run}(x)$, expressing that u is a proof of the proposition that $\mathbf{run}(x)$. Such a term u is called a *proof term* and plays a key role in representing the dynamic notion of contexts for resolving anaphora in DTS.

Anaphora resolution via underspecification In the following analysis, we mainly use two constructions, Σ-types and Π-types. Σ-type, written $(x : A) \times B$, is a generalization of product type $A \times B$. A term of type $(x : A) \times B$ is a pair (m, n) such that m has type A and n has type $B[m/x]$.[1] The projection functions π_1 and π_2 are defined so that $\pi_1(m, n) = m$ and $\pi_2(m, n) = n$. Σ-types can be used to represent existential quantification. For instance, *A man entered* is given the translation (6) in DTS.[2]

(6) $(u\colon (x : \mathtt{e}) \times \mathbf{man}(x)) \times \mathbf{enter}(\pi_1(u))$

Here u is a proof term of $(x : \mathtt{e}) \times \mathbf{man}(x)$, which is a pair of x having type $\mathtt{e}$ (entity) and a proof that x is a man. Thus, its first component (the entity x) can be picked up by the projection $\pi_1(u)$. The entire translation means that there is an entity x such that x is a man and x enters. For notational simplicity, we often abbreviate Σ-type of the form $(x : \mathtt{e}) \times A(x)$ as A^*, thus we write (6) as $(u : \mathbf{man}^*) \times \mathbf{enter}(\pi_1(u))$.

Π-type, $(x : A) \to B$ in our notation, is a generalization of function type $A \to B$. A term of type $(x : A) \to B$ is a function f such that for any term m of type A, $f(m)$ is of type $B[m/x]$. Π-type is used to represent universal quantification. Thus, *Every man entered* is given the translation in (7).

(7) $(u : \mathbf{man}^*) \to \mathbf{enter}(\pi_1(u))$

Note that when the variable x does not occur free in B, $(x : A) \times B$ and $(x : A) \to B$ can be written $A \times B$ and $A \to B$, respectively.

We illustrate how anaphora resolution works in DTS by the example *A man entered and he smiled*, which is given the following translation as an initial *underspecified* representation.

(8) $(v\colon (u : \mathbf{man}^*) \times \mathbf{enter}(\pi_1(u))) \times \mathbf{smile}(@_1\mathtt{e})$

In DTS, a pronoun is analyzed as an underspecified term @, possibly annotated with its type A, which we write $@A$. We assume that in the initial underspecified representation, each occurrence of underspecified term @ is assigned a mutually distinct index. In the above example, the pronoun *he* corresponds to $@_1\mathtt{e}$. This underspecified term searches for its antecedent of type $\mathtt{e}$ in the context represented as a proof term.

The initial step to resolve anaphora is *type checking*, which is a process to ensure that a given expression is a type (i.e. a well-formed proposition). This amounts to proving that it has type `type`, abbreviated as `t`. The formation rules (see Figure 1) tell us when a given expression has type `t`. In the case of (6), the goal is to prove that the representation in (6) has type `t`. In this case, no underspecified term appears, thus using the inference rules in Figure 1, we have the following *closed* derivation.

[1] Here and henceforth, $B[t/x]$ means the substitution of a term t for free occurrences of the variable x in the term B.

[2] We will provide an alternative analysis of indefinites later in this section.

(9) $$\dfrac{\dfrac{\dfrac{[x:\mathtt{e}]^1}{\mathbf{man}(x):\mathtt{t}}\ {\scriptstyle \mathbf{man}:\mathtt{e}\to\mathtt{t}}}{(x:\mathtt{e})\times\mathbf{man}(x):\mathtt{t}}\ {\scriptstyle \Sigma F,1} \qquad \dfrac{\dfrac{[u:(x:\mathtt{e})\times\mathbf{man}(x)]^2}{\pi_1(u):\mathtt{e}}\ {\scriptstyle \Sigma E}}{\mathbf{enter}(\pi_1(u)):\mathtt{t}}\ {\scriptstyle \mathbf{enter}:\mathtt{e}\to\mathtt{t}}}{(u:(x:\mathtt{e})\times\mathbf{man}(x))\times\mathbf{enter}(\pi_1(u)):\mathtt{t}}\ {\scriptstyle \Sigma F,2}$$

Here we assume that type assignments (signatures) such as $\mathtt{e}:\mathtt{t}$ and $\mathbf{enter}:\mathtt{e}\to\mathtt{t}$ are in the initial context and can be used as an axiom. To simplify derivations, we usually omit axioms and use the name of the predicate applied (possibly with its type) as a rule label.

If an initial representation contains an underspecified term @, the process of type checking tells us in what context the antecedent of the @-term can be found. For this purpose, we use the following rule:

(10) $$\dfrac{A:\mathtt{t} \quad A\ \mathtt{true}}{@_i A : A}\ {\scriptstyle @}$$

We use a judgement of the form $A\ \mathtt{true}$ to mean that there exists a term of type A; in other words, type A is inhabited. Using this rule, the type checking for (8) gives an *open* derivation as follows.

(11) $$\dfrac{\begin{array}{c}\vdots\ (9)\\ (u:\mathbf{man}^*)\times\mathbf{enter}(\pi_1(u)):\mathtt{t}\end{array} \qquad \dfrac{\dfrac{\dfrac{}{\mathtt{e}:\mathtt{t}}\ {\scriptstyle Ax} \quad \mathtt{e}\ \mathtt{true}}{@_1\mathtt{e}:\mathtt{e}}\ {\scriptstyle @}}{\mathbf{smile}(@_1\mathtt{e}):\mathtt{t}}\ {\scriptstyle \mathbf{smile}}}{(v:(u:\mathbf{man}^*)\times\mathbf{enter}(\pi_1(u)))\times\mathbf{smile}(@_1\mathtt{e}):\mathtt{t}}\ {\scriptstyle \Sigma F,1}$$

Here the derivation starts from the open premise $\mathtt{e}\ \mathtt{true}$. Once we prove $\mathtt{e}\ \mathtt{true}$ and find a witness for $@_i$, it becomes a closed derivation. To formalize this idea, we use the following rule for *@-elimination.*

(12) **@-elimination:** Let A be a term in which no @-term occurs. Then the derivation on the left can be transformed into the derivation on the right:

$$\begin{array}{c}\dfrac{\begin{array}{c}\vdots\\ A:\mathtt{t}\end{array} \quad \dfrac{\begin{array}{c}\vdots\ \mathcal{D}_2\\ u:A\end{array}}{A\ \mathtt{true}}}{@_i A : A}\ {\scriptstyle @}\\ \vdots\ \mathcal{D}_1\end{array} \quad \rightsquigarrow \quad \begin{array}{c}\vdots\ \mathcal{D}_2\\ u:A\\ \vdots\ \mathcal{D}_1[u/@_i A]\end{array}$$

This rule allows us to replace the underspecified term $@_i A$ with its witness u in the entire derivation.

To find a witness for an underspecified term @, we need to do proof search in a given local context. In the case of (11), the application of ΣF rule at the final step allows us to use a proof term for the left-side proposition, $(u:\mathbf{man}^*)\times\mathbf{enter}(\pi_1(u))$, to find a witness for $@_1\mathtt{e}$. It can be easily seen that one such witness is $\pi_1(\pi_1(v))$; in this case, we say $@_1\mathtt{e}$ is *bound* to $\pi_1(\pi_1(v))$.[3] Thus we have a closed derivation on the left below and it can be transformed to the derivation on the right by @-elimination.

$$\dfrac{\begin{array}{c}\vdots\ (9)\\ (u:\mathbf{man}^*)\times\mathbf{enter}(\pi_1(u)):\mathtt{t}\end{array} \quad \dfrac{\dfrac{\dfrac{}{\mathtt{e}:\mathtt{t}}\ {\scriptstyle Ax} \quad \dfrac{\dfrac{\dfrac{[v:(u:\mathbf{man}^*)\times\mathbf{enter}(\pi_1(u))]^1}{\pi_1(v):\mathbf{man}^*}\ {\scriptstyle \Sigma E}}{\pi_1(\pi_1(v)):\mathtt{e}}\ {\scriptstyle \Sigma E}}{\mathtt{e}\ \mathtt{true}}}{@_1\mathtt{e}:\mathtt{e}}\ {\scriptstyle @}}{\mathbf{smile}(@_1\mathtt{e}):\mathtt{t}}\ {\scriptstyle \mathbf{smile}}}{(v:(u:\mathbf{man}^*)\times\mathbf{enter}(\pi_1(u)))\times\mathbf{smile}(@_1\mathtt{e}):\mathtt{t}}\ {\scriptstyle \Sigma F,1} \quad \rightsquigarrow \quad \dfrac{\begin{array}{c}\vdots\ (9)\\ (u:\mathbf{man}^*)\times\mathbf{enter}(\pi_1(u)):\mathtt{t}\end{array} \quad \dfrac{\dfrac{\dfrac{[v:(u:\mathbf{man}^*)\times\mathbf{enter}(\pi_1(u))]^1}{\pi_1(v):\mathbf{man}^*}}{\pi_1(\pi_1(v)):\mathtt{e}}\ {\scriptstyle \Sigma E}}{\mathbf{smile}(\pi_1(\pi_1(u))):\mathtt{t}}\ {\scriptstyle \mathbf{smile}}}{(v:(u:\mathbf{man}^*)\times\mathbf{enter}(\pi_1(u)))\times\mathbf{smile}(\pi_1(\pi_1(u))):\mathtt{t}}\ {\scriptstyle \Sigma F,1}$$

The final representation can be read off from the bottom line of the derivation on the right.

(13) $(v:(u:\mathbf{man}^*)\times\mathbf{enter}(\pi_1(u)))\times\mathbf{smile}(\pi_1(\pi_1(v)))$

This is equivalent to saying that there is an entity x such that it satisfies $\mathbf{man}(x)$, $\mathbf{enter}(x)$, and $\mathbf{smile}(x)$.

Our analysis naturally accounts for the bound reading of (14a), whose translation is given in (14b).

(14) a. Every Englishman thinks he is a genius.

b. $(u:\mathbf{eng}^*)\to\mathbf{think}(\mathbf{genius}(@_1\mathtt{e}))(\pi_1(u))$

The derivation on the left shows the type checking with proof search to find a witness for $@_1\mathtt{e}$ in (14b).

[3] If the initial context (called *global context*) contains other possible antecedents, they give rise to different readings.

(15)
$$\dfrac{\dfrac{\dfrac{\dfrac{\dfrac{\dfrac{[u:\mathbf{eng}^*]^1}{\pi_1(u):\mathtt{e}}}{\mathtt{e\ true}}}{@_1\mathtt{e}:\mathtt{e}}@ \qquad}{\mathbf{genius}(@_1\mathtt{e}):\mathtt{t}}\,\text{genius} \quad \dfrac{[u:\mathbf{eng}^*]^1}{\pi_1(u):\mathtt{e}}}{\mathbf{think}(\mathbf{genius}(@_1\mathtt{e}))(\pi_1(u)):\mathtt{t}}\,\mathbf{think}:\mathtt{t}\to\mathtt{e}\to\mathtt{t}}{(u:\mathbf{eng}^*)\to\mathbf{think}(\mathbf{genius}(@_1\mathtt{e}))(\pi_1(u)):\mathtt{t}}\,\Sigma F,1 \quad\rightsquigarrow\quad \dfrac{\dfrac{\dfrac{\dfrac{[u:\mathbf{eng}^*]^1}{\pi_1(u):\mathtt{e}}}{\mathbf{genius}(\pi_1(u)):\mathtt{t}}\,\text{genius} \quad \dfrac{[u:\mathbf{eng}^*]^1}{\pi_1(u):\mathtt{e}}}{\mathbf{think}(\mathbf{genius}(\pi_1(u)))(\pi_1(u)):\mathtt{t}}\,\mathbf{think}:\mathtt{t}\to\mathtt{e}\to\mathtt{t}}{(u:\mathbf{eng}^*)\to\mathbf{think}(\mathbf{genius}(\pi_1(u)))(\pi_1(u)):\mathtt{t}}\,\Sigma F,1$$

Here the premise $\mathtt{e\ true}$ follows from the hypothesis $u:\mathbf{eng}^*$ licensed by the application of ΣF. Thus $@_1\mathtt{e}$ is bound to $\pi_1(u)$ and the @-term can be eliminated as shown in the derivation on the right. This yields the bound reading $(u:\mathbf{eng}^*)\to\mathbf{think}(\mathbf{genius}(\pi_1(u)))(\pi_1(u))$ for (14a), as desired.

An alternative treatment of indefinites In the classical version of DTS, pronouns and definites are translated as underspecified terms, while indefinites are not. Here we propose an alternative analysis that translates an indefinite to an underspecified term of the form $\#A$ where A is a Σ-type. This alternative analysis translates the sentence (6a) as follows (note that $\mathbf{man}^*$ is an abbreviation for $(x:\mathtt{e})\times\mathbf{man}(x)$):

(16) $\mathbf{enter}(\pi_1(\#\mathbf{man}^*))$

For underspecified terms $\#$, we use the following rule.[4]

(17) $\dfrac{A:\mathtt{t}}{\#A:A}\,\#$

The difference between $@_iA$ and $\#A$ is that while $@_iA$ searches for an antecedent of type A in a given local context via anaphora resolution, $\#A$ *introduces* an object of type A via the following rule for *$\#$-elimination*:

(18) **$\#$-elimination:** Let φ be a term containing $\#A$ as a subterm, where A is a type in which no @-term nor $\#$-term occurs. Suppose that we have a derivation of the form on the left, where $\varphi:\mathtt{t}$ is the first node that has type $\mathtt{t}$ and depends on $\#A:A$, i.e., no other judgement of the form $\psi:\mathtt{t}$ appears in $\mathcal{D}_2$. Then the derivation can be transformed into the one on the right:

$$\begin{array}{c}\vdots\,\mathcal{D}_1\\ \dfrac{A:\mathtt{t}}{\#A:A}\,\#\\ \vdots\,\mathcal{D}_2\\ \varphi:\mathtt{t}\end{array}\quad\rightsquigarrow\quad\dfrac{\begin{array}{c}\vdots\,\mathcal{D}_1\\ A:\mathtt{t}\end{array}\qquad\begin{array}{c}[u:A]^n\\ \vdots\,\mathcal{D}_2[u/\#A]\\ \varphi[u/\#A]:\mathtt{t}\end{array}}{(u:A)\times\varphi[u/\#A]:\mathtt{t}}\,\Sigma F,n$$

By this rule, if there is a branch containing an underspecified term $\#A$, one can close it by taking the existence of an object of type A as part of the asserted proposition represented as a Σ-type of the form $(u:A)\times\varphi[u/\#A]$, where $\varphi[u/\#A]$ is the expression obtained by replacing the occurrence of $\#A$ in φ by u. In the case of (16), the initial derivation shown on the left in (19) is transformed to the derivation on the right by $\#$-elimination, so we end up with the same representation as (6).

(19)
$$\dfrac{\dfrac{\dfrac{\dfrac{\dfrac{[x:\mathtt{e}]^1}{\mathbf{man}(x):\mathtt{t}}}{\mathbf{man}^*:\mathtt{t}}\,\Sigma F,1}{\#\mathbf{man}^*:\mathbf{man}^*}\,\#}{\pi_1(\#\mathbf{man}^*):\mathtt{e}}\,\Sigma E}{\mathbf{enter}(\pi_1(\#\mathbf{man}^*)):\mathtt{t}}\quad\rightsquigarrow\quad\dfrac{\dfrac{\dfrac{[x:\mathtt{e}]^1}{\mathbf{man}(x):\mathtt{t}}}{\mathbf{man}^*:\mathtt{t}}\,\Sigma F,1\qquad\dfrac{\dfrac{[u:\mathbf{man}^*]^1}{\pi_1(u):\mathtt{e}}\,\Sigma E}{\mathbf{enter}(\pi_1(u)):\mathtt{t}}}{(u:\mathbf{man}^*)\times\mathbf{enter}(\pi_1(u)):\mathtt{t}}\,\Sigma F,1$$

Thus $\#$-elimination allows us to eliminate a $\#$-term from a type and rewrite it to a Σ-type. For notational convenience, we write this transformation as $\mathbf{enter}(\pi_1(\#\mathbf{man}^*))\rightsquigarrow_\#(u:\mathbf{man}^*)\times\mathbf{enter}(\pi_1(u))$.

It should be clear from the above that DTS crucially makes use of underspecification in the interpretations of both pronouns and indefinites. We make the following two assumptions about the way underspecified terms are interpreted in the course of semantic composition:

[4] In this rule, $\#A:A$ must be understood as an open assumption depending on $A:\mathtt{t}$. In the sequent-style natural deduction, such a rule can be formulated more explicitly.

(20) a. **Ban on the duplication of underspecified terms:** In a well-formed semantic representation of DTS, an underspecified @-term with the same index can appear at most once.

b. **Normal form requirement on compositionally derived semantic terms:** At each step of semantic composition, the semantic term assigned to the derived linguistic expression is in β-normal form.

These restrictions can be thought of as embodying a general requirement that underspecification resolution is not totally unconstrained but is affected by the form of the sentences in which underspecified expressions occur. As such, these restrictions play key roles in the analysis of scope parallelism in the next section.

3 Analysis of the binding/scope parallelism

With the treatment of anaphora and indefinites introduced above, the interpretive parallelism exemplified by (1) and (2) falls out automatically as a consequence of the way underspecification is resolved in DTS. Unlike previous proposals (Asudeh and Crouch 2002; Steedman 2012), no extra assumption is needed beyond the simple restriction (20) on underspecification resolution introduced in the previous section.

We start with the pronominal binding case. To avoid the issue of possessives (which is itself a complex problem), we illustrate the analysis with the following example involving an embedded clause:

(21) Every Englishman thinks, and every American believes, that he is a genius.

One technical issue that needs to be addressed first is how to obtain the bound reading for the pronoun in the RNR'ed position to begin with. Note that given the prohibition on the duplication of underspecified terms in DTS, the simple derivation for (21) in (22) cannot yield the bound reading for the pronoun.[5]

(22)

$$\dfrac{\text{thinks}; \mathbf{think}; \mathrm{VP/S'} \qquad \begin{bmatrix}\varphi_1; \\ p; \mathrm{S'}\end{bmatrix}^1}{\text{thinks} \circ \varphi_1; \mathbf{think}(p); \mathrm{VP}}\ /\mathrm{E}$$

$$\dfrac{\begin{bmatrix}\varphi_2; \\ y; \\ \mathrm{NP}\end{bmatrix}^2 \qquad \text{thinks} \circ \varphi_1; \mathbf{think}(p); \mathrm{VP}}{\dfrac{\varphi_2 \circ \text{thinks} \circ \varphi_1; \mathbf{think}(p)(y); \mathrm{S}}{\lambda\varphi_2.\varphi_2 \circ \text{thinks} \circ \varphi_1; \lambda y.\mathbf{think}(p)(y); \mathrm{S{\restriction}NP}}\ {\restriction}\mathrm{I}^2}\ /\mathrm{E}$$

$$\dfrac{\lambda\sigma.\sigma(\text{every} \circ \text{Englishman}); \mathbf{V}_{\mathbf{eng}}; \mathrm{S{\restriction}(S{\restriction}NP)} \qquad \lambda\varphi_2.\varphi_2 \circ \text{thinks} \circ \varphi_1; \lambda y.\mathbf{think}(p)(y); \mathrm{S{\restriction}NP}}{\dfrac{\text{every} \circ \text{Englishman} \circ \text{thinks} \circ \varphi_1; \mathbf{V}_{\mathbf{eng}}(\lambda y.\mathbf{think}(p)(y)); \mathrm{S}}{\text{every} \circ \text{Englishman} \circ \text{thinks}; \lambda p.\mathbf{V}_{\mathbf{eng}}(\lambda y.\mathbf{think}(p)(y)); \mathrm{S/S'}}\ {\restriction}\mathrm{I}^1}\ {\restriction}\mathrm{E}$$

$$\dfrac{\text{and}; \lambda F\lambda G\lambda p.(v:G(p)) \times F(p); \mathrm{(X\backslash X)/X} \qquad \begin{matrix}\vdots \\ \text{every} \circ \text{American} \circ \text{believes}; \lambda q.\mathbf{V}_{\mathbf{am}}(\lambda y.\mathbf{believe}(q)(y)); \mathrm{S/S'}\end{matrix}}{\text{and} \circ \text{every} \circ \text{American} \circ \text{believes}; \lambda G\lambda p.(v:G(p)) \times \mathbf{V}_{\mathbf{am}}(\lambda y.\mathbf{believe}(p)(y)); \mathrm{(S/S')\backslash(S/S')}}\ /\mathrm{E}$$

$$\dfrac{\text{every} \circ \text{Englishman} \circ \text{thinks}; \lambda p.\mathbf{V}_{\mathbf{eng}}(\lambda y.\mathbf{think}(p)(y)); \mathrm{S/S'} \qquad \text{and} \circ \text{every} \circ \text{American} \circ \text{believes}; \ldots; \mathrm{(S/S')\backslash(S/S')}}{\text{every} \circ \text{Englishman} \circ \text{thinks} \circ \text{and} \circ \text{every} \circ \text{American} \circ \text{believes}; \lambda p.(v:\mathbf{V}_{\mathbf{eng}}(\lambda y.\mathbf{think}(p)(y))) \times \mathbf{V}_{\mathbf{am}}(\lambda y.\mathbf{believe}(p)(y)); \mathrm{S/S'}}\ \backslash\mathrm{E}$$

$$\dfrac{\ldots; \mathrm{S/S'} \qquad \text{that} \circ \text{he} \circ \text{is} \circ \text{a} \circ \text{genius}; \mathbf{gen}(@_1\mathbf{e}); \mathrm{S'}}{\text{every} \circ \text{Englishman} \circ \text{thinks} \circ \text{and} \circ \text{every} \circ \text{American} \circ \text{believes} \circ \text{that} \circ \text{he} \circ \text{is} \circ \text{a} \circ \text{genius}; \lambda p[(v:\mathbf{V}_{\mathbf{eng}}(\lambda y.\mathbf{think}(p)(y))) \times \mathbf{V}_{\mathbf{am}}(\lambda y.\mathbf{believe}(p)(y))](\mathbf{gen}(@_1\mathbf{e})); \mathrm{S}}\ /\mathrm{E}$$

$$\cdots\cdots\cdots\cdots\cdots\cdots$$

$$\lambda p[(v:(u:\mathbf{eng}^*) \to \mathbf{think}(p)(\pi_1(u))) \times ((u:\mathbf{am}^*) \to \mathbf{believe}(p)(\pi_1(u)))](\mathbf{gen}(@_1\mathbf{e}))$$

Here, for the pronoun in the RNR'ed S′ to be bound by the subject quantifiers in each conjunct, the term $\mathbf{gen}(@_1\mathbf{e})$ first needs to be substituted for variable p in each conjunct (from where the antecedent is syntactically visible, given the definition of anaphora resolution from section 2), but this is precisely the move that is prohibited by the 'no duplication of underspecified term' restriction.

This means that, in order to obtain the bound reading, we need a slightly more complex syntactic derivation involving (syntactic) type-lifting of both the RNR'ed material and the conjuncts. The effect in a nutshell is that, via type-lifting, we can ensure enough of the 'derivational structure' of the sentence to be present in the (beta-unreduced) semantic translation to identify the 'possible binder' of the pronoun before all the material is actually composed in the (surface) syntax. The derivation for the bound pronoun reading for (21) thus goes as in (23).

[5] We adopt the abbreviation $\mathbf{V}_{\mathbf{eng}} =_{def} \lambda P.[(u:\mathbf{eng}^*) \to P(\pi_1(u))]$, etc. These abbreviations are unpacked at the end of the derivation (via the step designated by the dotted line, which is not part of the syntactic derivation) for clarity of presentation.

(23)

$$\dfrac{\begin{matrix}\lambda\sigma.\sigma(\text{every} \circ \text{Englishman});\\ \mathbf{\forall_{eng}}; \mathrm{S}{\upharpoonright}(\mathrm{S}{\upharpoonright}\mathrm{NP})\end{matrix} \quad \dfrac{\dfrac{\begin{bmatrix}\varphi_3;\\ x; \mathrm{NP}\end{bmatrix}^3 \quad \dfrac{\text{thinks}; \mathbf{think}; \mathrm{VP/S'} \quad [\varphi_1; \mathscr{P}; (\mathrm{VP/S'})\backslash\mathrm{VP}]^1}{\text{thinks} \circ \varphi_1; \mathscr{P}(\mathbf{think}); \mathrm{VP}}\backslash\mathrm{E}}{\varphi_3 \circ \text{thinks} \circ \varphi_1; \mathscr{P}(\mathbf{think})(x); \mathrm{S}}\backslash\mathrm{E}}{\lambda\varphi_3.\varphi_3 \circ \text{thinks} \circ \varphi_1; \lambda x.\mathscr{P}(\mathbf{think})(x); \mathrm{S}{\upharpoonright}\mathrm{NP}}{\upharpoonright}\mathrm{I}^3}{\dfrac{\text{every} \circ \text{Englishman} \circ \text{thinks} \circ \varphi_1; \mathbf{\forall_{eng}}(\lambda x.\mathscr{P}(\mathbf{think})(x)); \mathrm{S}}{\text{every} \circ \text{Englishman} \circ \text{thinks}; \lambda\mathscr{P}.\mathbf{\forall_{eng}}(\lambda x.\mathscr{P}(\mathbf{think})(x)); \mathrm{S}/((\mathrm{VP/S'})\backslash\mathrm{VP})}/\mathrm{I}^1}{\upharpoonright}\mathrm{E}$$

$$\dfrac{\begin{matrix}\vdots\\ \text{every} \circ \text{Englishman} \circ \text{thinks} \circ \text{and} \circ\\ \text{every} \circ \text{American} \circ \text{believes};\\ \lambda\mathscr{P}.(v\!:\mathbf{\forall_{eng}}(\lambda x.\mathscr{P}(\mathbf{think})(x)))\\ \times(\mathbf{\forall_{am}}(\lambda x.\mathscr{P}(\mathbf{believe})(x)));\\ \mathrm{S}/((\mathrm{VP/S'})\backslash\mathrm{VP})\end{matrix} \quad \dfrac{\dfrac{\dfrac{\begin{bmatrix}\varphi_5;\\ x; \mathrm{NP}\end{bmatrix}^5 \quad \dfrac{[\varphi_4; \mathscr{R}; \mathrm{VP/S'}]^4 \quad \text{that} \circ \text{he} \circ \text{is} \circ \text{a} \circ \text{genius}; \mathbf{gen}(@_1\mathbf{e}); \mathrm{S'}}{\varphi_4 \circ \text{that} \circ \text{he} \circ \text{is} \circ \text{a} \circ \text{genius}; \mathscr{R}(\mathbf{gen}(@_1\mathbf{e})); \mathrm{VP}}/\mathrm{E}}{\varphi_5 \circ \varphi_4 \circ \text{that} \circ \text{he} \circ \text{is} \circ \text{a} \circ \text{genius}; \mathscr{R}(\mathbf{gen}(@_1\mathbf{e}))(x); \mathrm{S}}\backslash\mathrm{E}}{\varphi_4 \circ \text{that} \circ \text{he} \circ \text{is} \circ \text{a} \circ \text{genius}; \lambda x.\mathscr{R}(\mathbf{gen}(@_1\mathbf{e}))(x); \mathrm{VP}}{\upharpoonright}\mathrm{I}^5}{\text{that} \circ \text{he} \circ \text{is} \circ \text{a} \circ \text{genius}; \lambda\mathscr{R}\lambda x.\mathscr{R}(\mathbf{gen}(@_1\mathbf{e}))(x); (\mathrm{VP/S'})\backslash\mathrm{VP}}{\upharpoonright}\mathrm{I}^4}{\begin{matrix}\text{every} \circ \text{Englishman} \circ \text{thinks} \circ \text{and} \circ \text{every} \circ \text{American} \circ \text{believes} \circ \text{that} \circ \text{he} \circ \text{is} \circ \text{a} \circ \text{genius};\\ \lambda\mathscr{P}[(v\!:\mathbf{\forall_{eng}}(\lambda x.\mathscr{P}(\mathbf{think})(x))) \times (\mathbf{\forall_{am}}(\lambda x.\mathscr{P}(\mathbf{believe})(x)))](\lambda\mathscr{R}\lambda x.\mathscr{R}(\mathbf{gen}(@_1\mathbf{e}))(x)); \mathrm{S}\\ \cdots\cdots\cdots\cdots\cdots\cdots\cdots\cdots\cdots\cdots\cdots\cdots\cdots\cdots\cdots\cdots\cdots\\ \lambda\mathscr{P}[(v\!:(u\!:\mathbf{eng}^*) \to \mathscr{P}(\mathbf{think})(\pi_1(u))) \times ((u\!:\mathbf{am}^*) \to \mathscr{P}(\mathbf{believe})(\pi_1(u)))](\lambda\mathscr{R}\lambda x.\mathscr{R}(\mathbf{gen}(@_1\mathbf{e}))(x))\end{matrix}}/\mathrm{E}$$

Type checking for the semantic representation involves a branch to check the type of $\lambda\mathscr{R}\lambda x.\mathscr{R}(\mathbf{gen}(@_1\mathtt{e}))(x)$, which is shown on the left below. Here the assumption $\mathtt{e\ true}$ follows from the hypothesis $x : \mathtt{e}$ and thus by @-elimination we can replace $@_1\mathtt{e}$ with x throughout the derivation.

(24)

$$\dfrac{\dfrac{\dfrac{\dfrac{\dfrac{\dfrac{[x:\mathtt{e}]^2}{\mathtt{e\ true}}}{@_1\mathtt{e}:\mathtt{e}}@}{\mathbf{gen}(@_1\mathtt{e}):\mathtt{t}} \quad [x:\mathtt{e}]^2}{\mathscr{R}(\mathbf{gen}(@_1\mathtt{e}))(x):\mathtt{t}} \quad [\mathscr{R}:\mathtt{t}\to\mathtt{e}\to\mathtt{t}]^1}{\lambda x.\mathscr{R}(\mathbf{gen}(@_1\mathtt{e}))(x):\mathtt{e}\to\mathtt{t}}\Pi I,2}{\lambda\mathscr{R}\lambda x.\mathscr{R}(\mathbf{gen}(@_1\mathtt{e}))(x):(\mathtt{t}\to\mathtt{e}\to\mathtt{t})\to\mathtt{e}\to\mathtt{t}}\Pi I,1 \quad \rightsquigarrow \quad \dfrac{\dfrac{\dfrac{\dfrac{[x:\mathtt{e}]^2}{\mathbf{gen}(x):\mathtt{t}} \quad [x:\mathtt{e}]^2}{\mathscr{R}(\mathbf{gen}(x))(x):\mathtt{t}} \quad [\mathscr{R}:\mathtt{t}\to\mathtt{e}\to\mathtt{t}]^1}{\lambda x.\mathscr{R}(\mathbf{gen}(x))(x):\mathtt{e}\to\mathtt{t}}\Pi I,2}{\lambda\mathscr{R}\lambda x.\mathscr{R}(\mathbf{gen}(x))(x):(\mathtt{t}\to\mathtt{e}\to\mathtt{t})\to\mathtt{e}\to\mathtt{t}}\Pi I,1$$

Note crucially that here the underspecification for the pronoun term $@_1\mathtt{e}$ is resolved before the meaning contribution of the RNR'ed S′ which contains it as a subterm is copies into each conjunct via β-reduction. The underspecified term identifies the (λ-bound) subject x of the upstairs clause as its antecedent. After @-elimination and β-reduction, we obtain the final translation in (25), which corresponds to the parallel bound reading for the sentence.

(25) $\lambda\mathscr{P}[(v\!:(u\!:\mathbf{eng}^*) \to \mathscr{P}(\mathbf{think})(\pi_1(u))) \times ((u\!:\mathbf{am}^*) \to \mathscr{P}(\mathbf{believe})(\pi_1(u)))](\lambda\mathscr{R}\lambda x.\mathscr{R}(\mathbf{gen}(x))(x))$
$\twoheadrightarrow_\beta ((u\!:\mathbf{eng}^*) \to \mathbf{think}(\mathbf{gen}(\pi_1(u)))(\pi_1(u)))) \times ((u\!:\mathbf{am}^*) \to \mathbf{believe}(\mathbf{gen}(\pi_1(u)))(\pi_1(u))))$

For the parallel free pronoun reading, the simpler derivation in (22) would suffice. Since β-reduction is prohibited before underspecification resolution, type checking for the underspecified term searches for an appropriate antecedent in the global context (consisting of the previous linguistic discourse and extra-linguistic information). For concreteness, we assume that the previous utterance was *Bobby Fisher is a famous American chess player*, and that the judgement $\mathbf{bf} : \mathtt{e}$ is in the global context. The previous sentence thus provides an antecedent and $@_1\mathtt{e}$ in (22) is bound to $\mathbf{bf}$. By β-reducing the term after anaphora resolution, we obtain (26), where the pronoun refers to Bobby Fisher in each conjunct.

(26) $((u\!:\mathbf{eng}^*) \to \mathbf{think}(\mathbf{gen}(\mathbf{bf})(\pi_1(u)))) \times ((u\!:\mathbf{am}^*) \to \mathbf{believe}(\mathbf{gen}(\mathbf{bf}))(\pi_1(u))))$

The quantifier scope case is somewhat different at the level of technical implementations, but at the broader conceptual level, is essentially similar to the pronoun case in that interpretive parallelism falls out from the constraints pertaining to underspecification resolution in the derivation of compositional semantics. Note first that, unlike the case for @-terms, we don't need to ensure that the derivationally obtained local context is 'large enough' to contain the 'antecedent'. Thus, the following simple derivation suffices to yield both the wide-scope and narrow-scope readings for the RNR'ed indefinite:

(27)

$$\dfrac{\begin{matrix}\vdots\\ \text{every} \circ \text{boy} \circ \text{admires} \circ \text{and} \circ \text{every} \circ \text{girl} \circ \text{hates};\\ \lambda x.(v\!:\mathbf{\forall_{boy}}(\lambda y.\mathbf{admire}(x)(y))) \times (\mathbf{\forall_{girl}}(\lambda y.\mathbf{hate}(x)(y))); \mathrm{S/NP}\end{matrix} \quad \begin{matrix}\text{some} \circ \text{saxophonist};\\ \#\mathbf{sax}^*; \mathrm{NP}\end{matrix}}{\begin{matrix}\text{every} \circ \text{boy} \circ \text{admires} \circ \text{and} \circ \text{every} \circ \text{girl} \circ \text{hates} \circ \text{some} \circ \text{saxophonist};\\ \lambda x[(v\!:\mathbf{\forall_{boy}}(\lambda y.\mathbf{admire}(x)(y))) \times (\mathbf{\forall_{girl}}(\lambda y.\mathbf{hate}(x)(y)))](\#\mathbf{sax}^*); \mathrm{S}\\ \cdots\cdots\cdots\cdots\cdots\cdots\cdots\cdots\cdots\cdots\cdots\cdots\\ \lambda x[(v\!:(u\!:\mathbf{boy}^*) \to \mathbf{admire}(x)(\pi_1(u))) \times ((u\!:\mathbf{girl}^*) \to \mathbf{hate}(x)(\pi_1(u)))](\#\mathbf{sax}^*)\end{matrix}}$$

Since #-terms do not carry indices, in the case of indefinites, interpretive parallelism follows not from the ban on duplicating indexed underspecified terms (whose role was to ensure 'construal identity' in anaphora resolution), but from an interaction of the normal form requirement for derived semantic terms and the locality requirement on underspecification resolution encoded in the #-elimination rule (18). Specifically, there are two possible ways for resolving underspecification for the #-term in the semantic translation for the sentence obtained at the final line of (27). If we resolve underspecification before β-reducing the term, we obtain the wide scope reading for the indefinite as in (28):

(28) $\lambda x[(v:(u:\mathbf{boy}^*) \to \mathbf{admire}(x)(\pi_1(u))) \times ((u:\mathbf{girl}^*) \to \mathbf{hate}(x)(\pi_1(u)))](\#\mathbf{sax}^*)$
$\rightsquigarrow_{\#} (t:\mathbf{sax}^*) \times \lambda x[(v:(u:\mathbf{boy}^*) \to \mathbf{admire}(x)(\pi_1(u))) \times ((u:\mathbf{girl}^*) \to \mathbf{hate}(x)(\pi_1(u)))](\pi_1(t))$
$\to_\beta (t:\mathbf{sax}^*) \times [(v:(u:\mathbf{boy}^*) \to \mathbf{admire}(\pi_1(t))(\pi_1(u))) \times ((u:\mathbf{girl}^*) \to \mathbf{hate}(\pi_1(t))(\pi_1(u)))]$

If, on the other hand, we first β-reduce the term and then resolve underspecification, the Σ-type that has the existential force associated with the indefinite is introduced in the smallest local context in each conjunct, via (18). In this case, the distributive, narrow scope reading obtains for the sentence.

(29) $\lambda x[(v:(u:\mathbf{boy}^*) \to \mathbf{admire}(x)(\pi_1(u))) \times ((u:\mathbf{girl}^*) \to \mathbf{hate}(x)(\pi_1(u)))](\#\mathbf{sax}^*)$
$\to_\beta (v:(u:\mathbf{boy}^*) \to \mathbf{admire}(\#\mathbf{sax}^*)(\pi_1(u))) \times ((u:\mathbf{girl}^*) \to \mathbf{hate}(\#\mathbf{sax}^*)(\pi_1(u)))$
$\rightsquigarrow_{\#} (v:(u:\mathbf{boy}^*) \to (t:\mathbf{sax}^*) \times \mathbf{admire}(\pi_1(t))(\pi_1(u))) \times ((u:\mathbf{girl}^*) \to (t:\mathbf{sax}^*) \times \mathbf{hate}(\pi_1(t))(\pi_1(u)))$

One may wonder at this point why we impose the normal form requirement on compositionally derived semantic terms. To see why this requirement is needed, assume that no β-reduction takes place in the course of the derivataion, and, (as above) that once the semantic representation for the whole sentence is obtained, there is no restriction on the order of β-reduction and underspecification resolution for #-terms. The following translation would then be assigned to the sentence, and via the underspecification resolution in (30), a mixed scope reading would incorrectly be predicted to be available:

(30) $\lambda P \lambda Q \lambda x[(v:P(x)) \times Q(x)](\lambda y \mathbf{V}_{\mathbf{boy}}(\mathbf{admire}(y)))(\lambda z \mathbf{V}_{\mathbf{girl}}(\mathbf{hate}(z)))(\#\mathbf{sax}^*)$
$\to_\beta (v:\mathbf{V}_{\mathbf{boy}}(\mathbf{admire}(\#\mathbf{sax}^*))) \times \lambda z[\mathbf{V}_{\mathbf{girl}}(\mathbf{hate}(z))](\#\mathbf{sax}^*)$
$\rightsquigarrow_{\#} (v:\mathbf{V}_{\mathbf{boy}}((t:\mathbf{sax}^*) \times \mathbf{admire}(\pi_1(t)))) \times ((t:\mathbf{sax}^*) \times \lambda z[\mathbf{V}_{\mathbf{girl}}(\mathbf{hate}(z))](\pi_1(t)))$
$\to_\beta (v:\mathbf{V}_{\mathbf{boy}}((t:\mathbf{sax}^*) \times \mathbf{admire}(\pi_1(t)))) \times ((t:\mathbf{sax}^*) \times \mathbf{V}_{\mathbf{girl}}(\mathbf{hate}(\pi_1(t))))$

In short, assumption (20b) has the effect of eliminating unnecessary 'traces' of derivational history to make unavailable intermediate scope positions that do not reflect the surface form of the sentence.

Our proposal treats indefinites as underspecified terms and universals as true quantifiers, and in this respect, resembles the approach by Steedman (2012). Unlike Steedman's approach, which interleaves underspecification resolution with CCG syntactic combinatorics, our approach separates semantic underspecification resolution from syntax. Nonetheless, the similarity between the two is striking, and it is interesting to note that they both predict that mixed readings are available for examples involving indefinites as subjects and a universal quantifier in the RNR'ed position, such as the following:

(31) Some boy loves, and some girl detests, every saxophonist.

The judgments are somewhat subtle due to the independent pragmatic preference for parallel readings, but we follow Steedman (2012) in taking this prediction to be essentially correct.

One translation that our analysis can assign to (31) is the following:

(32) $\lambda \mathscr{P}[(u:(\lambda y[\mathscr{P}(\lambda x.\mathbf{love}(x)(y))](\#\mathbf{boy}))) \times \lambda z[\mathscr{P}(\lambda x.\mathbf{hate}(x)(z))](\#\mathbf{girl})](\mathbf{V}_{\mathbf{sax}})$

Here, β-conversion for the λ-bound variables y, z and $\mathscr{P}$ can take place in any order, and the relative scope between the subject indefinites and the object universal depends on the order of application of β-conversion and underspecification resolution for the two terms $\#\mathbf{boy}$ and $\#\mathbf{girl}$.

4 Conclusion and outlook

In this paper, we have proposed an analysis of the interpretive parallelism for anaphora and scope in the so-called Geach sentences involving right-node raising. In the proposed analysis, the parallel interpretation requirement on pronouns and indefinites in the shared right periphery is a consequence of the way underspecified terms are interpreted in the underspecification language that mediates the compositional semantic representation straightforwardly derived from the syntactic derivation and the fully resolved semantic representation that explicitly encodes all the relevant logical entailment relations. The natural next question is whether the present approach can be extended to the ellipsis cases. Preliminary results suggest a positive answer to this question, but a detailed analysis is a task for future research.

Acknowledgments

This work was supported by JSPS KAKENHI JP15K16732, the NINJAL collaborative research project 'Cross-linguistic Studies of Japanese Prosody and Grammar' and the OSU College of the Arts and Sciences Larger Grant.

References

Asudeh, A. and R. Crouch (2002). Derivational parallelism and ellipsis parallelism. In L. Mikkelsen and C. Potts (Eds.), *WCCFL 21 Proceedings*, Somerville, MA, pp. 1–14. Cascadilla Press.

Bekki, D. (2014). Representing anaphora with dependent types. In N. Asher and S. Soloviev (Eds.), *Logical Aspects of Computational Linguistics 2014*, Heidelberg, pp. 14–29. Springer.

Bekki, D. and K. Mineshima (2017). Context-passing and underspecification in Dependent Type Semantics. In S. Chatzikyriakidis and Z. Luo (Eds.), *Modern Perspectives in Type-Theoretical Semantics*, pp. 11–41. Heidelberg: Springer.

Fox, D. (2000). *Economy and Semantic Interpretation*. Cambridge, Mass.: MIT Press.

Geach, P. T. (1972). A program for syntax. In D. Davidson and G. H. Harman (Eds.), *Semantics of Natural Language*, pp. 483–497. Dordrecht: D. Reidel.

Hirschbühler, P. (1982). VP deletion and across-the-board quantifier scope. In J. Pustejovsky and P. Sells (Eds.), *Proceedings of the Twelfth Annual Meeting of the North Eastern Linguistic Society*, pp. 132–139. University of Massachusetts at Amherst.

Jacobson, P. (1999). Towards a variable-free semantics. *Linguistics and Philosophy 22*(2), 117–184.

Kubota, Y. and R. Levine (2012). Gapping as like-category coordination. In D. Béchet and A. Dikovsky (Eds.), *Logical Aspects of Computational Linguistics 2012*, Heidelberg, pp. 135–150. Springer.

Kubota, Y. and R. Levine (2015). Against ellipsis: Arguments for the direct licensing of 'non-canonical' coordinations. *Linguistics and Philosophy 38*(6), 521–576.

Martin-Löf, P. (1984). *Intuitionistic Type Theory*. Bibliopolis.

Puthawala, D. (2018). Stripping isn't so mysterious, or anomalous scope, either. In A. Foret, G. Kobele, and S. Pogodalla (Eds.), *Formal Grammar 2018*, pp. 102–120.

Steedman, M. (2012). *Taking Scope*. Cambridge, Mass.: MIT Press.

Translating a Fragment of Natural Deduction System for Natural Language into Modern Type Theory

Ivo Pezlar
The Czech Academy of Sciences, Institute of Philosophy
pezlar@flu.cas.cz

Abstract

In this paper, we investigate the possibility of translating a fragment of natural deduction system (NDS) for natural language semantics into modern type theory (MTT), originally suggested by Luo (2014). Our main goal will be to examine and translate the basic rules of NDS (namely, meta-rules, structural rules, identity rules, noun rules and rules for intersective and subsective adjectives) to MTT. Additionally, we will also consider some of their general features.

1 Introduction

In this paper, we will examine two proof-theoretic approaches to natural language semantics. Specifically, we will explore the possibility of embedding natural deduction systems (NDS, Francez 2015) into modern type theory (MTT, Chatzikyriakidis and Luo 2017b), originally hinted at by Luo (2014).

Our main goal will be to examine and try to translate the basic rules of NDS (namely, meta-rules, structural rules, identity rules, noun rules and rules for intersective and subsective adjectives) to MTT. Additionally, we will also consider some of their general features.

2 NDS and MTT: A Preliminary Overview

MTT is closely related to Martin-Löf's constructive type theory (Martin-Löf 1984) and it fully utilizes its rich type structures (dependent types, inductive types, ...). NDS is more similar to the standard logical approach based on Gentzen's natural deduction. In practice, this means that with NDS we are devising a purely proof-theoretic framework, but with MTT we are allowed more liberties due to its type-theoretic nature. This earned MTT some criticism from Francez, who regards MTT as 'a model-theoretic semantics, but one *constrained by proof-theoretic constraints*' (see Francez and Dyckhoff 2010, pp. 474–475). This point was not contested but rather embraced by Luo (see Luo 2014), who views his MTT as having both proof-theoretic and model-theoretic features (see Luo 2014, pp. 177–178).

The choice of a base system also dictates what will be the main vehicles for content: in MTT we work with judgements of the form $a : A$, where a is a so-called proof object (proof term, witness, justification, ...) and A a proposition/type, while in NDS we work with formulas (or (pseudo-)sentence in the case of natural language fragment). From a technical standpoint, probably the most important difference between judgements and formulas is that judgements have effective procedural content, i.e., they are decidable. More specifically, given a judgement $a : A$ we should be always able to compute whether a is an object of the type A. Consider e.g., the judgement $1 : Nat$, i.e., the judgement that 1 is a natural number. The number 1 is in constructive type theories usually defined simply as $s(0) : Nat$, i.e., as the successor of 0. This form alone tells us that 1 is indeed a natural number, since in MTT all natural numbers are either 0 or have the form $s(a)$ where a is a natural number.[1] This is not the case with

[1]This follows from the introduction rules for natural numbers. For a proper definition of natural numbers in MTT, see e.g., Martin-Löf (1984).

Proceedings of the IWCS 2019 Workshop on Computing Semantics with Types, Frames and Related Structures, pages 10–18
Gothenburg, Sweden, May 24, 2019.

formulas, which are generally undecidable. For example, suppose that $a \in P$ is a formula of predicate logic capturing the fact that a has some property P, more specifically that a is in the set P. Whether some element is a member of a set or not is, however, generally not decidable. Consequently, $a \in P$ is undecidable as well.[2] Other points of discord could be found as well. For example, if our translation of NDS into MTT succeeds, we lose some of the nice 'philosophical' properties of NDS (e.g., fewer ontological commitments).[3] On the other hand, if we are solely interested in formal semantics, this does not need to concern us.

So far we have discussed only the differences between NDS and MTT, but we can identify important similarities as well. The key intuition of proof-theoretic semantics that meanings are constituted via canonical proofs[4] is, of course, present in both systems. As Francez states:

> For compound sentences, sentential meanings are defined as the (contextualised) *collection of canonical derivations* [...]. This is very much in the spirit of the modern approach 'propositions as types' (for example, Martin-Löf 1984), the inhabitants of a type being the the proofs [...]. (Francez 2015, p. 46)

As expected, both systems rely on the standard scheme of introduction rules mirrored by the corresponding elimination rules. MTT adds to this mix, however, also formation rules and computation rules (also called equality rules), which can be understood as rules for assembling well-formed terms and for term reductions, respectively. Both frameworks also avoid the Fregean function-argument form of predication ($F(a)$) and move towards the more classical subject-predicate predication (S is P) reminiscent of Aristotelian logic. More specifically, NDS utilizes pseudo-sentences of the general form a isa A, while MTT operates with judgements of the general form $a : A$. NDS also relies on the so-called reification of meaning, which puts it apart from most PTS approaches, but closer to MTT:

> The approach I am proposing in this book is rather to conceive of PTS as providing an *explicit definition* of meanings by meaning-conferring rules. Thus, if ξ is some meaning bearing expression, PTS should provide some *proof-theoretic semantic value* of the form $[\![\xi]\!] =^{df.} \cdots$ as the meaning of ξ. I refer to this semantic value as a reified meaning. (Francez 2015, p. 7)

This reification is similar to MTT and its underlying conception of propositions as sets of proof objects. Assume that we have two proof objects $\lambda x.x$ and $\lambda y.y$ for the proposition $A \supset A$. These two proof objects differ only in the names of bound variables, i.e., they are α-equivalent. In MTT, we can express all this as $\lambda x.x : A \supset A$, $\lambda y.y : A \supset A$, and finally $\lambda x.x =_\alpha \lambda y.y : A \supset A$. Compare this with NDS and its expression $[\![A \supset A]\!]^{Ic}$ denoting the set of all I-canonical proofs of $A \supset A$. Since $\lambda x.x$ and $\lambda y.y$ are essentially understood as reified proofs or codes for proofs, we can see that both $\lambda x.x =_\alpha \lambda y.y : A \supset A$ and $[\![A \supset A]\!]^{Ic}$ capture a similar intuition.

3 From NDS to MTT

In our translation, we start with meta-rules (3.1), then we consider identity rules (3.2), rules for proper names (3.3), and finally we will examine rules for intersective and subsective adjectives (3.4). As we shall see, all the discussed NDS rules can be embedded into MTT semantics and justified either as admissible rules or derivable rules.

The translation method we utilize is based on the suggestion made by Luo (2014). Generally speaking, the translation method has two steps: 1) identifying the suitable expressions of NDS for the application of translation function $[\![\ ]\!]$ (a syntactic step), and 2) finding the appropriate translations in MTT

---

[2] Many other distinctions between formulas and judgements can be identified, but since it is a topic beyond the scope of this paper, we will not pursue it further.

[3] See Francez (2015), p. 9.

[4] A proof is canonical if and only if it ends with an application of an introduction rule. We call such proof an I-canonical proof (see Def. 1.5.8, Francez 2015, p. 36). In the framework of MTT, this corresponds to proof objects being in a canonical form, i.e., a form given to them by the corresponding introduction rules.

(a semantic step). As an simple example, suppose we have an expression Alice isa student, which is a proper sentence of NDS, hence we can apply the translation function $[\![\text{Alice isa student}]\!]$. As the corresponding translation in MTT, we get the judgement $Alice : Student$. Although the translation is not always as straightforward as Luo's quote might suggest, we will show that in general it can be successfully deployed for all the basic rules (meta-rules, identity rules, noun rules, adjective rules).

3.1 Meta-Rules

The meta-rules for NDS (see below) are intended to confer meaning of sentences from the natural language fragment containing only in/transitive verbs, determiner phrases with a singular noun, determiners 'every' and 'some' and a copula 'is' (see Francez 2015). The rules for determiners come in pairs of introduction rules (I-rules) and (generalized) elimination rules (E-rules) and they behave in accordance with the standard intuitionistic explanations of the corresponding quantifiers.

$$\frac{}{\Gamma, S \vdash S}\,(Ax) \qquad \frac{\Gamma, \mathbf{j} \text{ isa } X \vdash S[\mathbf{j}]}{\Gamma \vdash S[(\text{every } X)]}\,(eI) \qquad \frac{\Gamma \vdash \mathbf{j} \text{ isa } X \qquad \Gamma \vdash S[\mathbf{j}]}{\Gamma \vdash S[(\text{some } X)]}\,(sI)$$

$$\frac{\Gamma \vdash S[(\text{every } X)] \qquad \Gamma \vdash \mathbf{j} \text{ isa } X \qquad \Gamma, S[\mathbf{j}] \vdash S'}{\Gamma \vdash S'}\,(eE)$$

$$\frac{\Gamma \vdash S[(\text{some } X)] \qquad \Gamma, \mathbf{j} \text{ isa } X, S[\mathbf{j}] \vdash S'}{\Gamma \vdash S'}\,(sE)$$

where $\mathbf{j}$ is fresh for $\Gamma, S[\text{every } X]$ in (eI), and for $S[\text{some } X], S'$ in (sE).[5]

First, some additional explanations are in order: $\mathbf{j}$, X, and S are meta-variables for individual parameters (determiner phrases, ...), nouns (including compound nouns), and (affirmative) pseudo-sentences,[6] respectively, while isa serves as a copula. Furthermore, expression of the form $S[\mathbf{j}]$ means that $\mathbf{j}$ occupies a determiner phrase position in the sentence S. every and some are determiners (for more, see Francez 2015).

First, we present all the translated variants for meta-rules, then we add comments and examples.

$$\frac{}{[\![\Gamma]\!], [\![S]\!] \vdash [\![S]\!]}\,(Ax)' \qquad \frac{[\![\Gamma]\!], j : [\![X]\!] \vdash [\![S[j]]\!]}{[\![\Gamma]\!] \vdash [\![S[\forall([\![X]\!])]]\!]}\,(eI)' \qquad \frac{[\![\Gamma]\!] \vdash j : [\![X]\!] \qquad [\![\Gamma]\!] \vdash [\![S[j]]\!]}{[\![\Gamma]\!] \vdash [\![S[\exists([\![X]\!])]]\!]}\,(sI)'$$

$$\frac{\Gamma \vdash [\![S[\forall([\![X]\!])]]\!] \qquad [\![\Gamma]\!] \vdash j : [\![X]\!] \qquad [\![\Gamma]\!], [\![S[j]]\!] \vdash [\![S']\!]}{[\![\Gamma]\!] \vdash [\![S']\!]}\,(eE)'$$

$$\frac{[\![\Gamma]\!] \vdash [\![S[\exists([\![X]\!])]]\!] \qquad [\![\Gamma]\!], j : [\![X]\!], [\![S[j]]\!] \vdash [\![S']\!]}{[\![\Gamma]\!] \vdash [\![S']\!]}\,(sE)'$$

Comments. The rule $(Ax)'$ is justified by the structural rule assump from MTT. The rules $(eI)'$ and $(sI)'$ are justified by the rules Π-intro and Σ-intro (or more precisely, via $\forall$-intro and $\exists$-intro that are based upon them), respectively. Analogously for the rules $(eE)'$ and $(sE)'$. The context Γ from NDS, i.e., a finite list of formulas, is translated into a list of judgements. More specifically, in MTT, $\Gamma \vdash a : A$ is a hypothetical judgement properly unpacked as $a_1 : A, \ldots, a_n : A \vdash a : A$ where n is the number of assumptions in the context. The copula 'isa' is used for predication in NDS. In MTT, predication is achieved with the use of colon ':', so translating $\mathbf{j}$ isa X as $j : [\![X]\!]$ seems as a good fit. This decision dictates the rest of the translation: if we replace isa with :, then the left-hand side has to be some object and the right-hand side has to be its type. The most straightforward way to treat the determiner every

[5] Since we will not be interested here in the issue of quantifier scope ambiguity, we omit the corresponding explicit scope indicators from the rules. For example, the rule (sI) in its fully disclosed variant looks like $\frac{\Gamma, \mathbf{j} \text{ isa } X \vdash S[\mathbf{j}]}{\Gamma \vdash S[(\text{every } X)_{r(S[\mathbf{j}]+1)}]}\,(eI)$.

[6] A pseudo-sentence (of the object language) is a schematic sentences with occurrences of at least one parameter, e.g., $\mathbf{j}$ isa X. Example of a (pseudo-)sentence might be e.g., $\mathbf{j}$ isa student.

seems to be simply to take it as the universal quantifier $\forall$, which is defined in MTT via the Π type.[7] In other words, we will capture $S[(\textsf{every } X)]$ as sentential function over individual parameters, i.e., as an indexed family of types over the objects of type X. Analogously for the determiner some that can be treated via the Σ type.[8]

Examples. The following derivation from NDS:

$$\frac{\Gamma, \mathbf{j} \textsf{ isa girl} \vdash \mathbf{j} \textsf{ smiles}}{\Gamma \vdash \textsf{every girl smiles}} \ (eI)$$

gets as its MTT variant the following derivation:

$$\frac{\Gamma, j : Girl \vdash s(j) : Smiles(j)}{\Gamma \vdash \lambda j.s(j) : (\forall j : Girl) Smiles(j)} \ (eI)'$$

Note that in MTT, the noun girl is captured as the type $Girl$ and the predicate smiles as the dependent type $Smiles(j)$. Furthermore, note that the relationship between **j** and S in NDS, i.e., $S[\mathbf{j}]$, is captured in MTT by interpreting $S[\mathbf{j}]$ as a type of sentence (proposition) depending on the assumption $j : Girl$. We can also see that this formalization is in accord with Francez's own approach:

> A proof of $S[(\textsf{every } X)]$ is a function mapping each proof of **j** isa X (for an arbitrary fresh parameter **j**) into a proof of $S[\mathbf{j}]$. (Francez 2015, p. 247)

On our approach, the proof of $(\forall j : Girl) Smiles(j)$ is the proof object $\lambda j.s(j)$ which is a function (or rather a function name) that takes a proof object j and returns a proof object $s(j)$.[9]

As a more complicated example with a transitive verb, the NDS derivation:

$$\frac{\mathbf{k} \textsf{ isa boy} \qquad \dfrac{\Gamma, \mathbf{j} \textsf{ isa girl} \vdash \mathbf{j} \textsf{ loves } \mathbf{k}}{\Gamma \vdash \textsf{every girl loves } \mathbf{k}} \ (eI)}{\Gamma \vdash \textsf{every girl loves some boy}} \ (sI)$$

becomes:
$$\frac{k : Boy \qquad \dfrac{\Gamma, j : Girl, y : A \vdash l(j, y) : Loves(j, y)}{\Gamma, y : A \vdash \lambda j.l(j, y) : (\forall j : Girl) Loves(j, y)} \ (eI)'}{\Gamma \vdash (k, \lambda j.l(j, y)) : (\exists k : Boy)(\forall j : Girl) Loves(j, k)} \ (sI)'$$

And a derivations such as: $\dfrac{\Gamma, \mathbf{k} \textsf{ isa boy} \vdash \mathbf{j} \textsf{ loves } \mathbf{k}}{\Gamma \vdash \mathbf{j} \textsf{ loves every boy}} \ (eI)$ becomes:

$$\frac{\Gamma, k : Boy, x : A \vdash l(x, k) : Loves(x, k)}{\Gamma, x : A \vdash \lambda k.l(x, k) : (\forall k : Boy) Loves(x, k)} \ (eI)' .$$

3.2 Identity Rules

In the natural language fragment, Francez works with a set of rules determining the behaviour of the copula is, which is treated as 'a disguised identity' (Francez 2015, p. 250). Naturally, it behaves in the same way. The collection of rules is as follows:[10]

$$\frac{\Gamma, S[\mathbf{j}] \vdash S[\mathbf{k}]}{\Gamma \vdash \mathbf{j} \textsf{ is } \mathbf{k}} \ (isI) \qquad \frac{\Gamma \vdash \mathbf{j} \textsf{ is } \mathbf{k} \quad \Gamma \vdash S[\mathbf{j}]}{\Gamma \vdash S[\mathbf{k}]} \ (is\hat{E}) \qquad \frac{}{\Gamma \vdash \mathbf{j} \textsf{ is } \mathbf{j}} \ (is/r) \qquad \frac{\Gamma \vdash \mathbf{j} \textsf{ is } \mathbf{k}}{\Gamma \vdash \mathbf{k} \textsf{ is } \mathbf{j}} \ (is/s)$$

[7] Π type is essentially a Cartesian product of a family of sets.

[8] NDS also utilizes the structural rules of contraction and weakening, which correspond to multiple and vacuous discharge of assumptions in MTT.

[9] Note that since we are capturing **j** isa X as a judgement and not a proposition, it would make no sense speaking about its proof objects.

[10] We skip over the generalized variant (isE) (see Francez 2015, p. 250) and use only the derived version $(is\hat{E})$ presented above.

$$\frac{\Gamma \vdash \mathbf{j}\ \mathsf{is}\ \mathbf{k} \quad \Gamma \vdash \mathbf{k}\ \mathsf{is}\ \mathbf{l}}{\Gamma \vdash \mathbf{j}\ \mathsf{is}\ \mathbf{l}}\ (is/t)$$

Before we approach the translation of these rules, we have to address that in MTT there are two kinds of identity: *propositional* (or extensional) and *judgemental* (intensional, definitional). Probably the most important difference is that the judgemental identity, represented as $a = b : A$, is decidable, while the propositional identity, usually written as $Id(A, a, b)$, is not.[11] So what type of identity describe the rules above? If their were describing judgemental identity, then the translation of the reflexivity, symmetry and transitivity would be straightforward. For example, the MTT variant of $(is - sym)$ would be: $\frac{a = b : A}{b = a : A}$ symm , etc. However, given the fact that the identity rules of NDS have dedicated I- and E-rules, they seem to be describing propositional identity. In MTT, we cannot *introduce* judgemental identity in a way we would introduce e.g., some logical operator.[12]

The translated variants would be:

$$\frac{[\![\Gamma]\!], j = k : A, [\![S[j]]\!] \vdash [\![S[k]]\!]}{[\![\Gamma]\!] \vdash Id(A, j, k)}\ (isI)' \qquad \frac{[\![\Gamma]\!] \vdash Id(A, j, k) \quad [\![\Gamma]\!] \vdash [\![S[j]]\!]}{[\![\Gamma]\!] \vdash [\![S[k]]\!]}\ (is\hat{E})'$$

$$\frac{}{[\![\Gamma]\!] \vdash Id(A, j, j)}\ (is/r)' \qquad \frac{[\![\Gamma]\!] \vdash Id(A, j, k)}{[\![\Gamma]\!] \vdash Id(A, k, j)}\ (is/s)'$$

$$\frac{[\![\Gamma]\!] \vdash Id(A, j, k) \quad [\![\Gamma]\!] \vdash Id(A, k, l)}{[\![\Gamma]\!] \vdash Id(A, j, l)}\ (is/t)'$$

where A is the type of the objects j and k that we would use to represent the individual parameters. For example, if we have **j** isa girl in NDS, then we assume that $j : Girl$ in MTT.

Comments. Validity of the $(isI)'$ rule follows from the fact that, in general, from $a = b : A$ we can deduce $refl(A, a) : Id(A, a, b)$, which can be derived as a rule from Id-intro using substitution and set equality rules:

$$\frac{\dfrac{\Gamma, x : A \vdash Id(A, a, x) : type \qquad \Gamma \vdash a = b : A}{\Gamma \vdash Id(A, a, a) = Id(A, a, b)} \qquad \dfrac{\Gamma \vdash a : A}{\Gamma \vdash refl(A, a) : Id(A, a, a)}}{\Gamma \vdash refl(A, a) : Id(A, a, b)}$$

The rule $(is - refl)'$ is justified by the Id-intro rule. The rule $(is\hat{E})'$ is sanctioned by the Id-elim rule. With the constant $refl$ provided by the Id-intro rule, we can also prove symmetry and transitivity of the relation Id and supply the corresponding derived rules for symmetry:[13]

$$\frac{d : Id(A, a, b)}{symm(d) : Id(A, b, a)} \qquad \frac{d : Id(A, a, b) \qquad e : Id(A, b, c)}{trans(d, e) : Id(A, a, c)}$$

which in turn justify the rules $(is/s)'$ and $(is/t)'$, respectively.

3.3 Proper Names Rules

The I- and E-rules for proper names, which are ranged over by meta-variables N, M, are specified as follows (see Francez 2015, p. 251):

$$\frac{\Gamma \vdash \mathbf{j}\ \mathsf{is}\ N \qquad \Gamma \vdash S[\mathbf{j}]}{\Gamma \vdash S[N]}\ (nI) \qquad \frac{\Gamma \vdash S[N] \qquad \Gamma, \mathbf{j}\ \mathsf{is}\ N, S[\mathbf{j}] \vdash S'}{\Gamma \vdash S'}\ (nE)$$

[11] As a concrete example of this distinction, consider e.g., the difference between numbers $5 + 7$ and 12. While their are both extensionally equal (they both denote the number 12), they are not intensionally equal (they do not denote it in the same way). Alternatively, we can view this distinction as a difference between abstract objects and linguistic terms.

[12] Recall that $a = b : A$ is one of the basic kinds of MTT judgements.

[13] For proofs and definitions of the constants $symm$ and $trans$, see e.g., Nordström et al. (1990).

The translated variants will become:

$$\frac{[\![\Gamma]\!] \vdash Id(A,j,n) \quad [\![\Gamma]\!] \vdash [\![S[j]]\!]}{[\![\Gamma]\!] \vdash [\![S[n]]\!]} (nI)' \qquad \frac{[\![\Gamma]\!] \vdash [\![S[n]]\!] \quad [\![\Gamma]\!], Id(A,j,n), [\![S[j]]\!] \vdash [\![S']\!]}{[\![\Gamma]\!] \vdash [\![S']\!]} (nE)'$$

Comments. Similarly to the case above, we capture j is N via propositional identity. Furthermore, note that $(nI)'$ is essentially just a special case of Id-elim rule from MTT. More generally, it is an instance of the Leibniz's principle of the indiscernibility of identicals, which can be in MTT expressed as follows:

$$(\forall x : A)(\forall y : A)(\forall p : Id(A,x,y))B(x) \supset B(y).$$

Informally, it states that whenever we have two identical names, we can freely swap them in any sentence they appear. For its proof using the Id-elim rule, see e.g., Martin-Löf (1984). The $(nE)'$ rule is also justifiable via Id-elim.

Examples. As an example, we construct the derivation (8.3.35) (see Francez 2015, p. 251) establishing that:

Rachel isa girl, every girl smiles ⊢ Rachel smiles

which under our translation amounts to:

$$Rachel : Girl, \lambda x.s(x) : (\forall x : Girl)Smiles(x) \vdash s(Rachel) : Smiles(Rachel)$$

It can be derived as follows:

$$\frac{Rachel : Girl \qquad \dfrac{Id(Girl, r, Rachel) \qquad \dfrac{r : Girl \qquad \lambda x.s(x) : (\forall x : Girl)Smiles(x)}{s(r) : Smiles(r)} (e\hat{E})'}{s(Rachel) : Smiles(Rachel)} (nI)'}{s(Rachel) : Smiles(Rachel)} (nE)'$$

3.4 Adjectives

3.4.1 Intersective Adjectives

In this section, we examine and compare NDS and MTT approaches to intersective adjectives. We will take intersective adjectives as specified by adhering to the following two kinds of rules:

$$\frac{a \text{ is } Adj\ Noun}{a \text{ is } Adj} intA_1 \qquad \frac{a \text{ is } Adj\ Noun}{a \text{ is } Noun} intA_2$$

For example,

$$\frac{a \text{ is } black\ car}{a \text{ is } black} intA_1 \qquad \frac{a \text{ is } black\ car}{a \text{ is } car} intA_2$$

Hence, intersective adjectives are those adjectives that allow inferring from 'a is $Adj\ Noun$' that the underlying object of predication a possesses both its constituents separately: the noun $Noun$, i.e., 'a is $Noun$', as well as the intersective adjective Adj, i.e., 'a is Adj'. Observe that the compound $Adj\ Noun$ of intersective adjective and noun behaves similarly to the logical connective conjunction in standard natural deduction. More specifically, in natural deduction, conjunction has associated two elimination rules: $\frac{A \wedge B}{A} \wedge_1$-E and $\frac{A \wedge B}{B} \wedge_2$-E . These two rules correspond in their behaviour to rules $intA_1$ and $intA_1$. Elimination rules for conjunction allow deducing both its conjuncts A and B separately, and, analogously, rules for intersective adjectives allow deducing both its parts Adj and $Noun$. Hence, we could say that intersective adjectives preserve inferential content. We will utilize this fact later.

In NDS, intersective adjectives appear within *ground* pseudo-sentences of the form[14] j is A where A is a meta-variable for intersective adjective (see above). The corresponding rules are:

[14]Ground pseudo-sentences are pseudo-sentences that contain only parameters in every determiner phrase position. For example, j smiles. For more about ground pseudo-sentences, see Francez (2015), p. 245.

$$\frac{\Gamma \vdash \mathsf{j}\ \mathsf{isa}\ X \qquad \Gamma \vdash \mathsf{j}\ \mathsf{is}\ A}{\Gamma \vdash \mathsf{j}\ \mathsf{isa}\ A\ X}\,(adjI) \qquad \frac{\Gamma \vdash \mathsf{j}\ \mathsf{isa}\ A\ X \qquad \Gamma, \mathsf{j}\ \mathsf{isa}\ X, \mathsf{j}\ \mathsf{is}\ A \vdash S'}{\Gamma \vdash S'}\,(adjE)$$

From the rule $(adjE)$ we can obtain the following derived rules (see Francez 2015, p. 252):

$$\frac{\Gamma \vdash \mathsf{j}\ \mathsf{isa}\ A\ X}{\Gamma \vdash \mathsf{j}\ \mathsf{isa}\ X}\,(adj\hat{E}_1) \qquad \frac{\Gamma \vdash \mathsf{j}\ \mathsf{isa}\ A\ X}{\Gamma \vdash \mathsf{j}\ \mathsf{is}\ A}\,(adj\hat{E}_2)$$

It is easy to check that these two rules correspond to our general rules $intA_1$, $intA_2$ for intersective adjective and, consequently, to conjunction elimination rules. Furthermore, it now becomes clear that the original rule $(adjE)$ corresponds to the generalized conjunction elimination rule (see e.g., Negri et al. 2001): $\dfrac{A \wedge B \qquad \overset{[A \wedge B]}{C}}{C}\,\wedge\text{-GE}$. Before we get to the translation of the above rules, we will first discuss how adjectives are treated in MTT. Intersective adjectives are generally analyzed with Σ type, i.e., the same type that is also used for defining conjunction.[15] For example, the expression 'black car' would be captured as the type: $(\Sigma x : Car)Black(x)$, i.e., the type of cars that are black ($Black(x)$ is considered as a property/propositional function). The corresponding proof object is a pair (x, y) such that $x : Car$ and $y : Black(x)$, i.e., y is a justification (proof object) that x is black. Hence, common nouns are interpreted as distinct types, so we will get types of cars, animals, humans, etc. (so-called many-sorted type theory).[16]

The corresponding MTT introduction for $(adjI)$ would then be:[17]

$$\frac{\Gamma \vdash n : Noun \qquad \Gamma \vdash a : intAdj(x)}{\Gamma \vdash (n, a) : (\Sigma x : Noun)intAdj(x)}$$

We mentioned above that intersective adjectives should be conservative with respect to their inferential content. We can test this with projection functions fst and snd. Intuitively, fst and snd are operations that return the first and the second element of the proof object of the pair type $(\Sigma x : Noun)intAdj(x)$, respectively. For example, assume that we have the proof object p such that $p = (x, y)$ of $(\Sigma x : Car)Black(x)$, then $fst(p) = x : Car$ and $snd(p) = y : Black(fst(p))$.[18] The corresponding elimination rules will then be as follows:

$$\frac{\Gamma \vdash c : (\Sigma x : Noun)intAdj(x)}{fst(c) : Noun}\,(adj\hat{E}_1)' \qquad \frac{\Gamma \vdash c : (\Sigma x : Noun)intAdj(x)}{snd(c) : intAdj(x)}\,(adj\hat{E}_2)'$$

The projections fst and snd can be defined using the non-canonical constant E (brought by Σ-elim rule) in the following manner: $fst(c) = E(c, (x, y)x)$ and $snd(c) = E(c, (x, y)y)$, respectively.

Now, we can finally get to the translation of the rules themselves (we skip the generalized elimination variant):

$$\frac{[\![\Gamma]\!] \vdash j : [\![X]\!] \quad [\![\Gamma]\!] \vdash k : [\![A]\!]}{[\![\Gamma]\!] \vdash (j, k) : [\![A\ X]\!]}\,(adjI)' \quad \frac{[\![\Gamma]\!] \vdash j : [\![A\ X]\!]}{[\![\Gamma]\!] \vdash snd(j) : [\![A]\!]}\,(adj\hat{E}_1)' \quad \frac{[\![\Gamma]\!] \vdash j : [\![A\ X]\!]}{[\![\Gamma]\!] \vdash fst(j) : [\![X]\!]}\,(adj\hat{E}_2)'$$

Comments. As discussed above, the rules for intersective adjectives are justified by the corresponding Σ type rules.

Examples. The following NDS derivation (see Francez 2015, p. 252): $\dfrac{\mathsf{j}\ \mathsf{isa}\ Y \qquad \dfrac{\mathsf{j}\ \mathsf{isa}\ A\ X}{\mathsf{j}\ \mathsf{is}\ A}\,(adj\hat{E}_2)}{\mathsf{j}\ \mathsf{isa}\ A\ Y}\,(adjI)$

becomes: $\dfrac{k : [\![Y]\!] \qquad \dfrac{j : [\![A\ X]\!]}{snd(j) : [\![A]\!]}\,(adj\hat{E}_2)'}{(k, snd(j)) : [\![A\ Y]\!]}\,(adjI)'$

[15]Compare with Ranta (1994), pp. 34–35. However, it is important to note that in order for this formalization to work, subtyping has to be adopted as well. See Luo (2012).

[16]Hence, e.g., a sentence 'Alice is a girl' will be understood as stating that Alice is an object of type girl, not as stating that predicate girl is applied to the individual Alice.

[17]Note that in MTT the relation between noun and adjective is handled via the Σ type, while in NDS it is achieved by the fact that both predications 'isa X' and 'is A' share the same parameter j.

[18]As we can see, our initial rules $intA_1$ and $intA_2$ correspond to rules for left and right conjunction elimination defined via projections fst, snd, respectively.

3.4.2 Subsective Adjectives

We specify subsective adjectives by the following two rules:

$$\frac{a \text{ is } Adj\ Noun}{a \text{ is } Noun}\ subA_1 \qquad \frac{a \text{ is } Adj\ Noun}{a \text{ is } Adj_N}\ subA_2$$

For example,

$$\frac{a \text{ is } large\ mouse}{a \text{ is } mouse}\ intA_1 \qquad \frac{a \text{ is } large\ mouse}{a \text{ is } large_m}\ intA_2$$

Hence, subsective adjectives allow us to infer from 'a is $Adj\ Noun$' that the underlying object of predication a possesses both its constituents separately: the noun $Noun$, i.e., 'a is $Noun$', as well as the adjective Adj with the proviso it was relativized w.r.t $Noun$., i.e., 'a is Adj_N'. Thus, e.g., 'a is $large_m$' from the example above can be read as 'a is something large assuming mouse-largeness scale'. Analogously to intersective adjectives, we can see that the compound containing a subsective adjective and a noun behaves similarly to the logical connective conjunction.

In NDS, the rules for subsective adjectives are as follows (we omit the generalized elimination rules; Francez 2017):

$$\frac{\Gamma \vdash \mathbf{j} \text{ isa } X \quad \Gamma \vdash \mathbf{j} \text{ is } A_X}{\Gamma \vdash \mathbf{j} \text{ isa } A\ X}\ (subAI) \qquad \frac{\Gamma \vdash \mathbf{j} \text{ isa } A\ X}{\Gamma \vdash \mathbf{j} \text{ isa } X}\ (subAG\hat{E}_1) \qquad \frac{\Gamma \vdash \mathbf{j} \text{ isa } A\ X}{\Gamma \vdash \mathbf{j} \text{ isa } A_X}\ (subAG\hat{E}_2)$$

The crucial part for the translaton is the premise $\Gamma \vdash \mathbf{j}$ isa A_X in $(subAI)$ rule, which captures the fact that **j** is A only under the assumption that **j** isa X. Specifically, A_X is a family of adjectives over the set of nouns X. Hence, in effect, it makes the meaning of A dependent on the meaning of X. In other words, the meaning of A is restricted only to a certain class of nouns X. So we will have a different types of largeness: e.g., large human, large insect, large mammal, etc.

As Francez describes it:

> The unfolding of the adjectives can be seen as a purely formal devise to parameterize a subsective adjective: A_X is just a family of adjectives originating from A and parameterized by nouns X. The entailments in (4.14) are the basis for the revised I/E-rules for subsective adjectives. [...] The explicit parameterization replaces the dependency in the original rules. (Francez 2017, pp. 12–13)

In MTT, we can capture this dependency by making the whole type of subsective adjectives range over the X, i.e., (common) nouns. Thus its type will be $\forall\alpha : X.(\alpha \to Prop)$ (see Chatzikyriakidis and Luo 2013, Chatzikyriakidis and Luo 2017a). After the translation, we get:

$$\frac{[\![\Gamma]\!] \vdash j : [\![X]\!] \quad [\![\Gamma]\!] \vdash j : [\![A_X]\!]}{[\![\Gamma]\!] \vdash j : [\![A\ X]\!]}\ (subAI)' \qquad \frac{[\![\Gamma]\!] \vdash j : [\![A\ X]\!]}{[\![\Gamma]\!] \vdash j : [\![X]\!]}\ (subAG\hat{E}_1)' \qquad \frac{[\![\Gamma]\!] \vdash j : [\![A\ X]\!]}{[\![\Gamma]\!] \vdash j : [\![A_X]\!]}\ (subAG\hat{E}_2)'$$

Comments. Rules are justified by the corresponding Σ type rules.
Examples. The following NDS derivation (see Francez 2017, p. 12):

$$\frac{\mathbf{j} \text{ isa elephant} \qquad \mathbf{j} \text{ is small}_{\text{elephant}}}{\mathbf{j} \text{ isa small elephant}}$$

becomes:

$$\frac{\Gamma \vdash j : Elephant \qquad \Gamma \vdash k : Small_E(j)}{\Gamma \vdash (j,k) : (\Sigma j : Elephant)Small_E(j)}\ (subAI)'$$

where $Small_E$ denotes the fact that we use 'elephant-smallness' of type: $Elephant \to Prop$. Note that we cannot derive that there is something small (corresponding to $snd(l) : Small(fst(l))$), only that we have something small w.r.t. an elephant scale.

Acknowledgements. Work on this paper was supported by grant nr. 19-12420S from the Czech Science Foundation, GA ČR.

References

Chatzikyriakidis, S. and Z. Luo (2013). Adjectives in a Modern Type-Theoretical Setting. pp. 159–174. Springer, Berlin, Heidelberg.

Chatzikyriakidis, S. and Z. Luo (2017a). Adjectival and Adverbial Modification: The View from Modern Type Theories. *Journal of Logic, Language and Information 26*(1), 45–88.

Chatzikyriakidis, S. and Z. Luo (2017b). *Modern Perspectives in Type-Theoretical Semantics*. Springer Publishing Company, Incorporated.

Francez, N. (2015). *Proof-theoretic Semantics*. College Publications.

Francez, N. (2017). A Proof-Theoretic Semantics for Adjectival Modification. *Journal of Logic, Language and Information 26*(1), 21–43.

Francez, N. and R. Dyckhoff (2010). Proof-Theoretic Semantics for a Natural Language Fragment. *Linguistics and Philosophy 33*(6), 447–477.

Luo, Z. (2012). Formal semantics in modern type theories with coercive subtyping. *Linguistics and Philosophy 35*(6), 491–513.

Luo, Z. (2014). Formal Semantics in Modern Type Theories: Is It Model-Theoretic, Proof-Theoretic, or Both? In N. Asher and S. Soloviev (Eds.), *Logical Aspects of Computational Linguistics: 8th International Conference, LACL 2014, Toulouse, France, June 18-20, 2014. Proceedings*, Berlin, Heidelberg, pp. 177–188. Springer Berlin Heidelberg.

Martin-Löf, P. (1984). *Intuitionistic type theory*. Studies in proof theory. Bibliopolis.

Negri, S., J. von Plato, and A. Ranta (2001). *Structural Proof Theory*. Cambridge University Press.

Nordström, B., K. Petersson, and J. M. Smith (1990). *Programming in Martin-Löf's type theory: an introduction*. International series of monographs on computer science. Clarendon Press.

Ranta, A. (1994). *Type-theoretical Grammar*. Indices. Clarendon Press.

Modeling the Induced Action Alternation and the Caused-Motion Construction with Tree Adjoining Grammar (TAG) and Semantic Frames

Esther Seyffarth
Heinrich Heine University Düsseldorf
Düsseldorf, Germany
esther.seyffarth@hhu.de

Abstract

The induced action alternation and the caused-motion construction are two phenomena that allow English verbs to be interpreted as motion-causing events. This is possible when a verb is used with a direct object and a directional phrase, even when the verb does not lexically signify causativity or motion, as in "Sylvia laughed Mary off the stage". While participation in the induced action alternation is a lexical property of certain verbs, the caused-motion construction is not anchored in the lexicon. We model both phenomena with XMG-2 and use the TuLiPA parser to create compositional semantic frames for example sentences. We show how such frames represent the key differences between these two phenomena at the syntax-semantics interface, and how TAG can be used to derive distinct analyses for them.

1 Introduction

Verbs and their semantics generally play an important role in determining the semantics of English sentences. In many cases, the meaning of an event-denoting sentence can be derived by identifying the verb's syntactic arguments and assigning them to specific participant slots in the verb's semantic frame, thus creating a frame that represents the meaning of the whole sentence. However, the presence or absence of slot fillers is not the only way in which the semantics of a verb depends on its syntactic environment. The induced action alternation and the caused-motion construction are examples of phenomena in which certain syntactic structures can enrich the semantics of the observed verbs in a systematic way.

In this paper, we discuss the overlap of possible syntactic structures licensed by these two phenomena, draw attention to differences in the way they assign semantic frames to sentences, and present a TAG model written in XMG-2 that can parse input sentences and derive their semantics correctly. While participation in the induced action alternation is a lexical property of certain verbs and thus has to be specified for each participating verb in our grammar, the caused-motion construction can apply to all verbs that fulfill the constraints imposed by the construction, and is thus not anchored in the lexicon.

We use XMG-2 to model the constraints on frame unification that are required to generate the different frames licensed by the phenomena. We explore the phenomena from a perspective focused on modeling their key differences, and leave the implementation of edge cases to future work (see Section 5). This work contributes to research on verb alternations and constructions by showing how similar meanings can be generated by them, while pointing out important differences in the results and the underlying processes. This is also a step towards a better understanding of the alternation and the construction in the context of practical applications like semantic role labeling, where sentences involving the phenomena need to be analysed correctly in order to successfully model their meaning.

To our knowledge, this is the first work to deal with these two phenomena in a TAG setting.

Proceedings of the IWCS 2019 Workshop on Computing Semantics with Types, Frames and Related Structures, pages 19–27
Gothenburg, Sweden, May 24, 2019.

2 The Induced Action Alternation and the Caused-Motion Construction

This paper is concerned with differences between two phenomena at the syntax-semantics interface that license causative interpretations by different means. While verb alternations apply to specific sets of verbs in a language and allow these verbs to express their semantic arguments in particular syntactic forms (Levin, 1993), constructions are "form-meaning correspondences that exist *independently of particular verbs*" (Goldberg, 1995, emphasis added).

The induced action alternation (Levin, 1993) is a verb alternation that allows participating verbs to occur either intransitively or transitively, where the transitive use introduces a cause to the event (examples taken from Levin, 1993, p. 31):

(1) a. Sylvia jumped the horse over the fence.
    b. The horse jumped over the fence.

Sentence (1-a) can be paraphrased as "Sylvia caused the horse to jump over the fence". Here, the verb *jump* describes the action or behavior of the syntactic object, whereas in sentence (1-b), it describes the action or behavior of the syntactic subject.

When an English verb does not participate in the induced-action alternation, it may still be used to express a causative meaning. The caused-motion construction (Goldberg, 1995) allows sentences like the following to be interpreted:

(2) Sylvia hit the horse into the barn.

Sentence (2) can be paraphrased as "Sylvia hit the horse, and thereby caused the horse to move into the barn". Here, the verb *hit* describes the action of the syntactic subject, and the directional phrase *into the barn* describes a motion of the syntactic object that results from the action of the syntactic subject.

The caused-motion construction can also be used with intransitive verbs and verbs that do not lexically encode motion. Combining a verb with a direct object and a directional phrase can result in a caused-motion reading that is independent of the lexical meaning of the verb, as in (3), which can be paraphrased as "By laughing, Sylvia caused Mary to move off the stage".

(3) Sylvia laughed Mary off the stage.

In sentences involving the induced action alternation, the verb describes the action or behavior of the syntactic object. In contrast to this, sentences involving the caused-motion construction express the behavior of the syntactic subject in the verb, and the motion of the syntactic object in the directional phrase (often realized in the form of a PP, as in "off the stage", or an adverb, as in "away").

This paper is concerned with a type of sentence structure that is licensed by both phenomena. In both cases, the verb can occur together with a direct object and a directional phrase. When the verb in a sentence participates in the alternation, it is interpreted analogously to (1-a). If this reading is not available, the sentence can be interpreted analogously to (2) and (3). Constraints on the construction have been discussed in the literature, for instance in Goldberg (1995); Goldberg and Jackendoff (2004); Oyón (2007); Cervel (2009). Crucially, participation in the alternation is a lexical property of certain verbs, while the construction can productively apply to any verb, as long as that verb fulfills the constraints imposed by the construction. This means that sentences like (1-a) can also be interpreted in the caused-motion reading. We discuss the available analyses for sentences like this in the course of the paper.

One possible test for the distinction between the alternation and the construction is their behavior when the direct object and/or the directional phrase are deleted. For verbs in the induced action alternation, like *jump*, each of the sentences (4-a) - (4-c) is felicitous and interpretable, while non-alternating verbs only allow structures like (4-d) if they are intransitive (like *laugh*) and/or (4-e) if they are transitive (like *hit*). (4-f) is infelicitous for verbs that do not lexically encode motion or directedness. Note that (4-a) and (4-c) express that it is Sylvia who moves over the fence, whereas the horse is the moving entity in (4-b).

(4) a. Sylvia jumped.
 b. Sylvia jumped the horse.
 c. Sylvia jumped over the fence.
 d. Sylvia laughed. / *Sylvia hit.
 e. *Sylvia laughed Mary. / Sylvia hit Mary.
 f. *Sylvia laughed off the stage.

3 Modeling with XMG-2

We present an XMG-2 model that can be used to derive the available readings of sentences like those discussed above. XMG (eXtensible MetaGrammar, Crabbé et al. 2013) is a system for designing metagrammars that can be compiled into natural-language grammars. We use XMG-2 (Petitjean et al., 2016) to create a TAG fragment (Tree Adjoining Grammar, Joshi and Schabes 1997) that encodes the syntax and semantics of the sentence types discussed here. How XMG-2 generates compositional semantic frames is laid out in Lichte and Petitjean (2015). After compiling the metagrammar, we use TuLiPA (an open-source parsing environment by Kallmeyer et al., 2008) to parse input sentences and generate their frames (Arps and Petitjean, 2018).

The semantic frames for a sentence are generated based on the frames of the lexical items in the sentence and the unification constraints encoded in the metagrammar. This is inspired by Kallmeyer and Osswald (2014), who present a model for directed motion expressions and the dative alternation.

We aim for a grammar fragment that allows and disallows sentences according to the judgments given for the examples in (4). We achieve this by specifying the semantic frames for the lexical items that are involved and providing different mechanisms for the derivation of compositional semantic frames. We mark each lexical item in our grammar with the syntactic environments in which it can occur. The syntactic trees assign frames to input sentences. This allows us to parse not only the causative sentences, but also more basic cases, like "Sylvia laughed" or "The horse jumped over the fence", in accordance with the judgments in (4).

Fig. 1 presents the semantic frames we assume for the sentences (1-a) and (3).[1] Both phenomena add a causative reading to a sentence whose verb does not lexically express causativity.

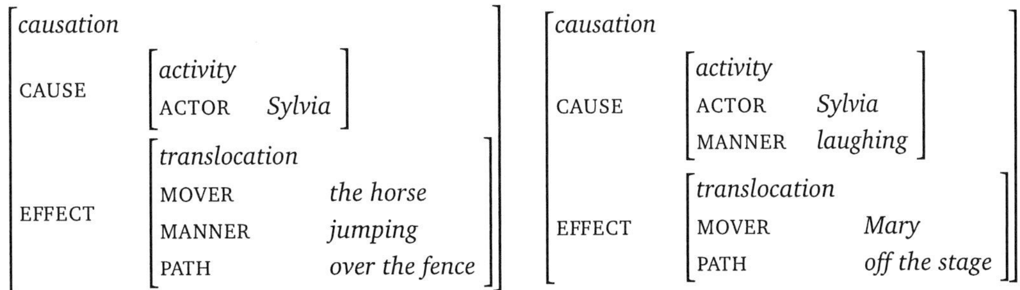

Figure 1: Event frames for (1-a) Sylvia jumped the horse over the fence (left, induced action alternation) and (3) Sylvia laughed Mary off the stage (right, caused-motion construction).

In (1-a), the manner in which Sylvia causes the horse to jump over the fence is not explicitly stated. This is reflected in the CAUSE subframe on the left in Fig. 1, where no MANNER attribute is given. The alternation observed here can only apply to a specific subset of English verbs. Therefore, we include in our grammar a dedicated tree for this sentence structure that is associated with a causation frame, and allow alternating verbs, like *jump*, to anchor that tree. Note that a verb's participation in the alternation must be made explicit in the grammar fragment for this analysis to be derived.

[1] Our representation of the meanings of "over" and "off" is simplified due to space and time limitations.

In (3), Sylvia's action is specified by the verb, *laugh*. Here, the manner in which Mary leaves the stage (running, walking, jumping, etc.) is not explicitly stated. This is reflected in the EFFECT subframe, which does not contain a MANNER attribute. Because the caused-motion construction exists independently of individual verbs, we let verbs like *laugh* or *hit* anchor regular intransitive/transitive trees; the tree for the caused-motion construction is a possible shape these trees can take, provided the syntactic structure is compatible. Furthermore, the participants in a given sentence must be semantically compatible with the slots of the causative frame, e.g., the ACTOR must be an agentive entity, and the MOVER must be an entity that can be caused to move. We do not impose any restrictions as to whether the MOVER has to belong to a type that can move by itself (like a horse), or a type that cannot move by itself (like a ball).

To design a metagrammar that can generate causation frames as in Fig. 1, we implement the following modules: (i) The **morph** file contains a morphological lexicon that connects word forms to the lemmas they belong to. We need this to parse inflected word forms, such as *jumped*. (ii) The **lemma** file contains a lexicon that connects known lemmas to their lexical frames. These are the "building blocks" that will be used to derive frames for full sentences. (iii) The **frame** file defines the type hierarchy and the frames that encode the lexical meaning of the lemmas, e.g. for the verb *jump*. (iv) Finally, the **syntax** file defines the syntactic trees for sentences. Where new frames arise compositionally from the syntactic structure, due to a verb alternation or a construction, the definition of that tree includes the appropriate frame and specifies which syntactic arguments will be used to fill the slots of the semantic frame. For a more detailed description of how these modules interact during parsing, see Arps and Petitjean (2018).

The trees that are generated for our input sentences during parsing assign different semantic frames to the sentences, depending on whether the verb in question participates in the induced action alternation. If it does, the frame will resemble the left side of Fig. 1; if not, it will resemble the right side.

Since the caused-motion construction is productive, it is conceivable that a conflict between these analyses may arise. This would be the case when a verb that participates in the induced action alternation is used in a way meant to realize the frame on the right of Fig. 1, not the one on the left. When parsing such a sentence, the frame for the induced action reading will be derived as expected. The frame for the caused-motion reading, where the verb is understood as applying to the syntactic subject, may however be available as an alternative interpretation. For instance, one might construe a situation in which Sylvia is jumping up and down in a way that scares the horse, causing it to move over the fence; in this case, the sentence (1-a) may be read as an example of the caused-motion construction.

This is why we allow all sentences that involve compatible lexical items to generate the semantic frame for the caused-motion construction. By explicitly marking verbs that participate in the induced action alternation, we ensure that TuLiPA will generate both analyses wherever appropriate.

3.1 Grammar Excerpts

As mentioned above, our grammar fragment consists of a **morph** file, a **lemma** file, a **frame** file and a **syntax** file. Examples from the files are presented in this section. The full grammar is available at `https://github.com/ojahnn/caused-motion-xmg`.

3.1.1 The `frame` File

The **frame** file contains a type hierarchy and the lexical frames for the frame-evoking items in our grammar. Since we are concerned with a grammar fragment for a specific set of phenomena, we use a small set of types and specify only a small number of attribute constraints.

Lexical frames for proper names, such as *Sylvia*, include the specification that the frame is of type `person`, as well as the corresponding value for the `name` attribute. Non-human agentive entities, such as *horse*, are given the type `actor`, as well as an attribute `kind` that describes them further. Similarly, non-animate entities such as *fence* are given the type `physical-entity`, with a `kind` attribute that describes them further. These are greatly simplified frame structures because our focus here is on the behavior of verbs and their influence on the structure of the derived event frames.

In our grammar fragment, we use directional phrases in the form of a set of prepositions. Since the semantic structure of prepositions like *over* is nontrivial, we opt for a simplified frame structure here, too. The prepositions in our grammar fragment are of type `path` and are described further by the value of their `trajectory` attribute. Because trajectories are typically understood in relation to a landmark, a `landmark` attribute is added when a PP is parsed (see e.g. Fig. 4).

Finally, the lexical frames for the verbs in our grammar fragment are given the type `activity` and distinguished further by the value of their `manner` attribute.

The frame hierarchy and type constraints, as well as examples for the kinds of frames mentioned above, are given in Fig. 2.

```
frame-types = {activity, physical_object, person, name,
        actor, mover, causation, manner, translocation,
        landmark, path, trajectory, kind}

frame-constraints = {
        physical_object -> kind: +,
        activity -> actor: +,
        person ->  name: + }
```

```
class FrameSylvia
declare ?X0
{    <frame>{
       ?X0[person,
          name: Sylvia]
 }; <iface>{
     [i=?X0]
}}
```

```
class FrameFence
export ?X0
declare ?X0
{    <frame>{
     ?X0[physical_object,
        kind: fence]
 }; <iface>{
     [i=?X0]
 }}
```

```
class FrameOver
export ?X0
declare ?X0
{    <frame>{
       ?X0[path,
          trajectory: over]
 }; <iface>{
     [i=?X0]
 }}
```

```
class FrameLaugh
export ?X0
declare ?X0
{    <frame>{
       ?X0[activity,
        manner: laughing]
 }; <iface>{
     [e=?X0]
 }}
```

Figure 2: Excerpts from the frame file. Type hierarchy and frame constraints (top left); frame for a proper name (top right); frame for a physical object (bottom left); frame for a preposition (bottom middle); frame for a verb (bottom right). The `iface` feature allows unification of lexical and compositional frames.

3.1.2 The `lemma` and `syntax` Files

Our **lemma** file specifies the sentence trees that can be anchored by each verb. For instance, the verb *laugh* can anchor intransitive sentences, which are covered by the tree named `n0V` in our **syntax** file. The verb *dance* can anchor intransitive sentences with or without directional phrases, so we connect it to the `n0V` tree as well as the `n0Vpp` tree, which is for verbs that lexically express motion.

The set of trees that can be anchored by the verb *jump* is where the induced action alternation comes into play. The verb can be used intransitively with or without a directional phrase; but unlike *laugh* or *dance*, it can also be used with a direct object and a directional phrase to trigger the induced action alternation. We encode this by letting this verb anchor the `n0V` and `n0Vpp` trees, as well as a special tree, `n0Vn1pp_actioninducing`. This is necessary because verbs in the alternation express their semantic arguments in different syntactic slots, compared to sentences with non-alternating verbs. The effect of the `n0Vn1pp_actioninducing` tree is that the verb frame defined in the frame file is "wrapped" in a causative frame that assigns the syntactic arguments to their semantic slots, as given in Fig. 1.

The caused-motion construction is triggered whenever a verb like *laugh* or *hit*, which cannot anchor the `n0Vn1pp_actioninducing` tree, is observed in the same syntactic environment (with a direct object and a directional phrase).[2] These cases are served by one of the possible realizations of the `n0V` tree, which is called `alphanx0Vnx1pp_motioncausing`. Its effect is to "wrap" the verb frame into a new, constructionally generated `causation` frame. Sentences that involve these verbs, but do not have the

[2]Note that some verbs, such as *imagine* or *prefer*, should not be assigned an `actor` attribute and can thus easily be excluded from anchoring this tree by way of additional type constraints in the frame file.

syntactic structure that triggers the caused-motion construction, are realized by the other realization of the `n0V` tree, `alphanx0V`.

All other words in our grammar fragment are also connected to appropriate elementary trees. This allows phrases like NPs and PPs to be derived from the corresponding token sequences, and the NPs and PPs can then be adjoined or substituted into the sentence trees described above.

Fig. 3 displays some example trees and shows that the construction can be applied to any activity verb in our grammar that can anchor simple intransitive trees, while the induced action frame can only be derived for those verbs that are lexically specified to anchor the corresponding tree.

```
class n0V
{ alphanx0V[] | alphanx0Vn1pp_motioncausing[] }
```

```
class n0Vpp
import Subject[] directedverb[]
declare ?X ?Y ?F
{<iface>{[cat=v, e=?F]};
 <frame>{?F[translocation,
            actor:?X,
            mover:?X,
            path:?Y]}
}
```

```
class alphanx0V
import Subject[] BareVerbProjection[]
declare ?F ?X
{<iface>{[cat=v, e=?F]};
 <frame>{?F[activity,
            actor:?X]}
}
```

```
class alphanx0Vn1pp_actioninducing
import Subject[] actioninducingverb[]
{<iface>{[cat=v, e=?G]};
 <frame>{[causation,
          cause:
              [activity,
               actor:?X],
          effect:
              ?G[translocation,
                 mover:?Z,
                 actor:?Z,
                 path:?Y]
  ]}}
```

```
class alphanx0Vn1pp_motioncausing
import Subject[] motioncausingverb[]
{<iface>{[e=?G]};
 <frame>{[causation,
          cause:
              ?G[activity,
                 actor:?X],
          effect:
              [translocation,
               mover:?Z,
               path:?Y]
  ]}}
```

Figure 3: Excerpts from the syntax file. The `n0V` tree has two realizations (top row). Trees with frames for intransitive sentences with PP (middle left) and without PP (middle right); trees with frames for transitive sentences with PP in alternation and construction reading (bottom left, bottom right). The `iface` feature allows unification of derived frame and lexical frames. The imported trees carry exclusively syntactic information.

4 Parsing With TuLiPA

Once the metagrammar is compiled, we use TuLiPA to check whether the sentences are correctly analyzed as specified in Fig. 1. When processing one of the input sentences, TuLiPA will look up the correct lemma for each observed word form; select possible lexical frames for the given lemmas; derive possible syntactic trees for the sentence; and generate a frame that represents the meaning of the full sentence. For sentences with a direct object and a directional PP, a causation frame will be generated, with the subframes for cause and effect filled as appropriate for the observed verb.

Fig. 4 shows one analysis generated by TuLiPA for the input sentence (1-a). The sentence licenses two different frames, since both readings are possible. The alternative reading is shown in Fig. 5.

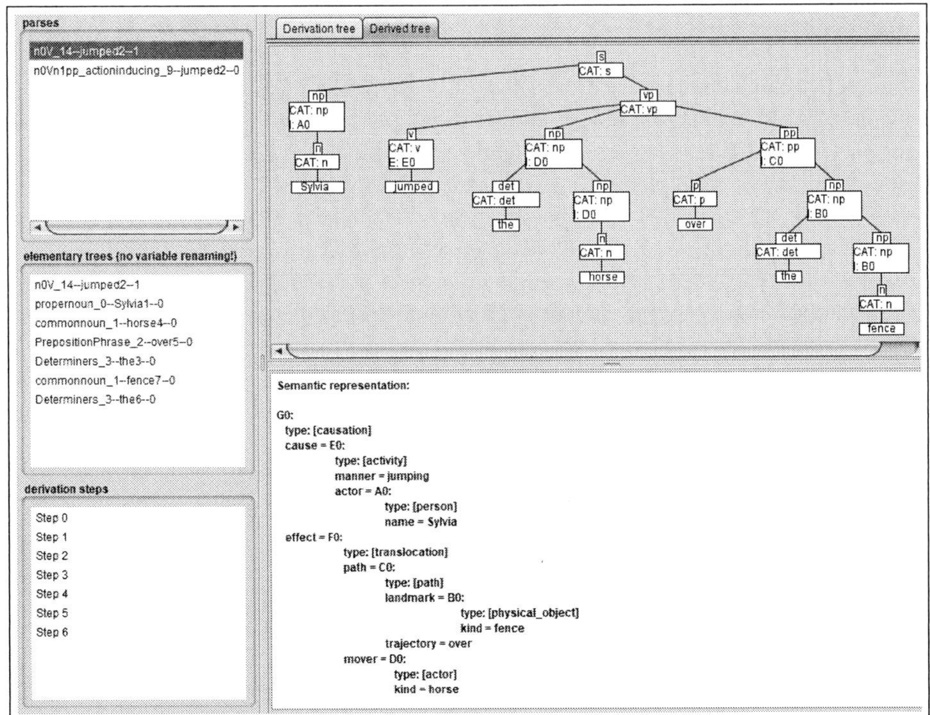

Figure 4: First TuLiPA output for sentence (1-a): Caused-motion reading. This analysis generates the frame associated with the paraphrase "By jumping, Sylvia caused the horse to move over the fence".

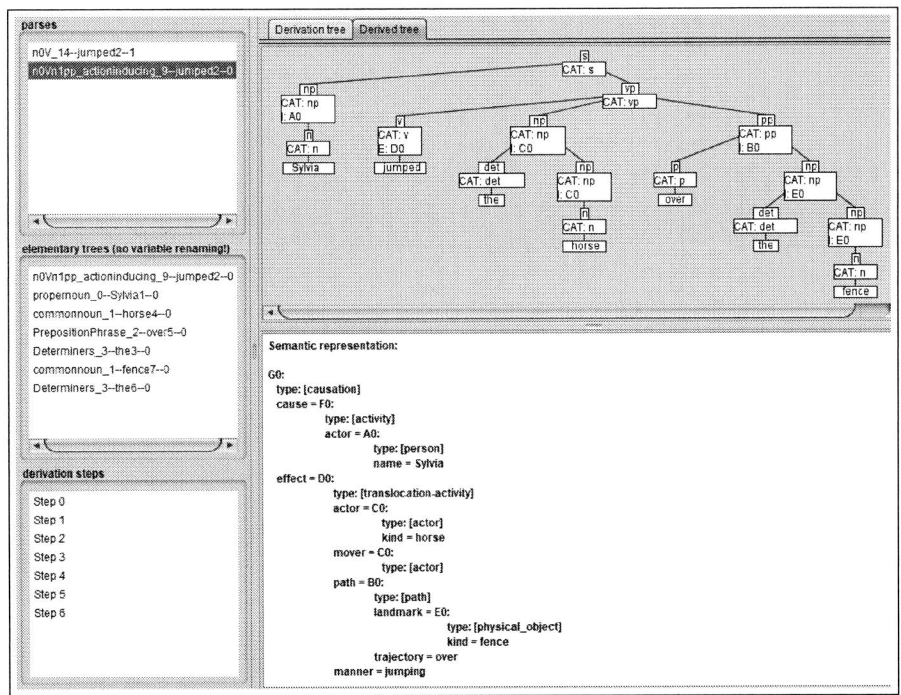

Figure 5: Second TuLiPA output for sentence (1-a): Induced-action reading. This analysis generates the same syntactic tree as shown in Fig. 4, but assigns a different frame to the sentence. This is the case because "jump" is marked in our grammar as participating in the induced action alternation.

5 Conclusion

The induced action alternation and the caused-motion construction are two different ways to use English verbs in a causative way, even when they do not lexically encode causation. We discuss the semantic frames that arise from different syntactic environments for each of these phenomena in Section 3.

We show how the two different types of semantic frames presented in Fig. 1 can be generated for input sentences using XMG-2. We also show that our model allows TuLiPA to provide more than one analysis for sentences that can be construed as examples of *both* phenomena.

Our analysis can be extended to reflect subtle differences in the interpretations of a range of possible usages of the caused-motion construction, as well as closely related constructions. Goldberg and Jackendoff (2004) treat the caused-motion construction as a "subconstruction of the resultative" (p. 535), which also includes other patterns at the syntax-semantics interface. Sentences that employ these related constructions can have the same syntactic structures as the ones discussed in this paper, but be associated with frames that are only distantly related to the frames we discuss here. A possible topic of future work is an extension of our grammar fragment so that it can handle these partially-related cases as well.

Goldberg and Jackendoff (2004) and Cervel (2009) discuss edge cases of the resultative and caused-motion construction that follow different constraints regarding selectional preferences; metaphorical readings are also often an option. The following examples (taken from Goldberg and Jackendoff 2004) illustrate part of the range of usages licensed by the construction:

(5) a. Bill walked himself into a coma.
    b. Bill followed the road into the forest.
    c. Aliza wiggled her tooth loose.
    d. Sara caught a plane to New York.
    e. Ray flew the coastal route to Buffalo.

With some additions, the grammar fragment would be able to analyze the sentences in (5).

To parse sentences like (5-a), reflexive pronouns can be added to the grammar fragment. As this example illustrates the resultative construction, the type constraints on the construction's frame may need to be modified, since "into a coma" is not a physical translocation, but a change of state.

In (5-b), unlike the sentences discussed in previous sections, the subject is the mover (it is Bill who is moving, not the road); the derivation of a causative frame could be prevented, for instance, by blocking the verb *follow* from anchoring trees that are associated with a caused-motion meaning. This could be done by giving *follow* a type that is specified to be incompatible with the caused-motion construction. Then, a different tree can be defined in the syntax file such that the frames derived for sentences like this are not causation frames.

Sentence (5-c) requires a refinement of the constraints that currently only allow directional phrases: For now, the grammar handles prepositional phrases, but it can easily be extended to also allow adverbs like *loose*. Like sentence (5-a), this sentence also expresses a change-of-state meaning, and the frame for this kind of sentence should be generated accordingly.

Sentences (5-d) and (5-e) seem to block the constructional interpretation we discuss above, because the prepositional phrases are part of the respective NPs, instead of being part of the VP.[3] The grammar needs to be extended to recognize such syntactic structures, so that frames similar to the one for sentence (5-b) can be created.

While further work is needed to enable the grammar fragment to parse these kinds of sentences, we have shown that TAG is well-suited to represent the two phenomena at the syntax-semantics interface that we have discussed. The XMG-2 framework allows us to neatly separate lexical meaning from constructional meaning. It can also provide more than one analysis if necessary; this is the case, for instance, when a sentence can be construed as exemplifying both the alternation and the construction.

[3]Sentence (5-e) seems to allow analyses that are analogous to either that of sentence (5-b) or that of sentence (5-e), so both syntactic trees and both frames should be made available to TuLiPa.

References

Arps, D. and S. Petitjean (2018). A Parser for LTAG and Frame Semantics. In *Proceedings of the Eleventh International Conference on Language Resources and Evaluation (LREC-2018)*, Miyazaki, Japan, pp. 7.

Cervel, M. S. P. n. (2009, November). Constraints on Subsumption in the Caused-Motion Construction. *Language Sciences 31*(6), 740–765.

Crabbé, B., D. Duchier, C. Gardent, J. Roux, and Y. Parmentier (2013). XMG: eXtensible MetaGrammar. *Computational Linguistics 39*(3), 591–629.

Goldberg, A. E. (1995). *Constructions: A Construction Grammar Approach to Argument Structure.* University of Chicago Press.

Goldberg, A. E. and R. Jackendoff (2004). The English Resultative as a Family of Constructions. *Language 80*(3), 532–568.

Joshi, A. K. and Y. Schabes (1997). Tree-Adjoining Grammars. In G. Rozenberg and A. Salomaa (Eds.), *Handbook of Formal Languages: Volume 3 Beyond Words*, pp. 69–123. Berlin, Heidelberg: Springer Berlin Heidelberg.

Kallmeyer, L., T. Lichte, W. Maier, Y. Parmentier, J. Dellert, and K. Evang (2008, August). TuLiPA: Towards a Multi-Formalism Parsing Environment for Grammar Engineering. In *Coling 2008: Proceedings of the Workshop on Grammar Engineering Across Frameworks*, pp. 1–8. Coling 2008 Organizing Committee.

Kallmeyer, L. and R. Osswald (2014). Syntax-Driven Semantic Frame Composition in Lexicalized Tree Adjoining Grammars. *Journal of Language Modelling 1*(2), 267–330.

Levin, B. (1993). *English Verb Classes and Alternations: A Preliminary Investigation.* University of Chicago press.

Lichte, T. and S. Petitjean (2015, July). Implementing Semantic Frames as Typed Feature Structures with XMG. *Journal of Language Modelling 3*(1), 185.

Oyón, A. L. (2007, January). Semantic Constraints on the Caused-Motion Construction. *Epos : Revista de filología 0*(23), 167.

Petitjean, S., D. Duchier, and Y. Parmentier (2016). XMG 2: Describing Description Languages. In M. Amblard, P. de Groote, S. Pogodalla, and C. Retoré (Eds.), *Logical Aspects of Computational Linguistics. Celebrating 20 Years of LACL (1996–2016)*, Lecture Notes in Computer Science, pp. 255–272. Springer Berlin Heidelberg.

Complex event representation in a typed feature structure implementation of Role and Reference Grammar

Erika Bellingham
University at Buffalo
ebelling@buffalo.edu

Abstract

Role and Reference Grammar (RRG) (Foley and Van Valin, 1984; Van Valin and LaPolla, 1997; Van Valin, 2005) is typologically general, semantically-driven syntactic framework. A major focus of RRG is a fine-grained typology of form-to-meaning mapping, emphasizing the syntactic and semantic structure of complex event descriptions. I introduce a constraint-based typed feature structure variant of RRG which exploits RRG's semantically-motivated syntactic backbone: the Layered Structure of the Clause (LSC). Each layer in the LSC is represented as a subtype of *sign*, and the unique combination of syntactic and semantic properties possessed by each layer is captured by a set of constraints on the appropriate *sign* subtype. Sentences are incrementally built up from predicates (represented semantically as event frames) to propositions using constructions to pass and combine information through the different layers (and juncture types) in the LSC. An English fragment of this constraint-based RRG is implemented using the Attribute Logic Engine (Carpenter, 1992).

1 Introduction

Role and Reference Grammar (RRG) offers a typologically motivated constructional approach to grammar, in which semantics plays a very significant role in syntactic structure. RRG's semantically motivated structural backbone, the Layered Structure of the Clause (LSC), offers several key advantages for capturing fine-grained semantic properties of classes of linguistic structures, particularly for complex sentences with multiple verbal elements. Semantic modifiers (adjuncts), as well as grammatical operators (e.g. tense, aspect, modals, negation), each apply to a specific layer of the clause, with the layer of application predicting both the position of the operator/modifier relative to the predicate (the nucleus of the clause), and the semantic scope of the operator/modifier. Complex event descriptions involving multiple verbal predicates vary in terms of their degree of both syntactic integration and semantic cohesion. The syntactic and semantic structures are isomorphically related to such a degree that an important conceptual property of the overall event representation - whether the event is represented as a single conceptual event (versus multiple conceptual events) - can be predicted based on the syntactic packaging.

The major effort towards formalizing RRG (Kallmeyer et al., 2013; Kallmeyer and Osswald, 2017; Osswald and Kallmeyer, 2018) uses the building blocks provided by Tree Adjoining Grammar (TAG) (Joshi and Schabes, 1997), with modified operations for combining trees. This paper introduces an alternative formalization possibility: a constraint-based variant of RRG, in which the layers in the LSC are implemented as typed feature structures. The focus is on building the backbone of syntactic and semantic representations to produce complex event representations that exploit the form-to-meaning mapping properties captured by the LSC, rather than on broad coverage of all syntactic possibilities. Drawing from Sign-based Construction Grammar (Sag, 2012), constructions are represented as typed feature structures with syntactic and semantic components. Events and entities are represented in a typed hierarchy of semantic frames, while the layers in the LSC are represented as subtypes of *sign*. Sentences are incrementally built from predicates using constructions to pass information between layers in the LSC.

Unification-based typed feature structure grammars (Carpenter, 1992) are mathematically well understood, computationally implementable and therefore easily testable, and are compatible with con-

Proceedings of the IWCS 2019 Workshop on Computing Semantics with Types, Frames and Related Structures, pages 28–36
Gothenburg, Sweden, May 24, 2019.

struction grammars. A fragment an English grammar using the proposed constraint-based RRG is implemented with the Attribute Logic Engine (ALE) (Carpenter and Penn, 2001), a Prolog implementation of the formalism in Carpenter (1992). The paper is structured as follows. Section 2 summarizes the relevant components of Role and Reference Grammar, focusing on RRG's Layered Structure of the Clause. Section 3 briefly discusses unification-based construction grammars, and Section 4 introduces this constraint-based variant of RRG. The ALE implementation is discussed in Section 5.

2 The Layered Structure of the Clause in RRG

Syntactic structure in RRG is built around abstract syntactic categories with semantic correlates: the layers in the Layered Structure of the Clause. The LSC is based on two apparently universal contrasts in the structure of natural languages: (1) predicating elements versus non-predicating elements, and (2) arguments versus non-arguments. Predicating elements (canonically verbs) are contained within **nuclei**, predicating elements plus their arguments are contained within **cores**, (most) non-arguments (adjuncts) are contained within the **core periphery**, and cores plus their peripheries are contained within the **clause**. Each layer is compatible with certain types of grammatical operators (Section 2.1) and semantic modifiers (Section 2.2): these operators or modifiers scope over a particular layer, which becomes especially relevant when considering the structure and interpretation of complex event descriptions (Section 2.3).

2.1 Grammatical operators

Grammatical categories (e.g. tense, aspect, modality, negation) are modelled in RRG as 'operators', each of which may apply only to a specific layer in the LSC. Not all languages have all operators: Standard German lacks grammatical aspect, English lacks grammatical evidentiality, Yucatec Maya lacks grammatical tense, and so on. Nuclear operators (e.g. aspect) modify something about the event/action/state without reference to any of the event participants, and therefore have scope only over the nucleus. Core operators (e.g. deontic modals) modify some property of the involvement of the participants in the event, and have scope over the core. Clausal operators, which modify propositions, fall into two distinct categories: tense and status operators situation the proposition expressed by the clause temporally and along the irrealis-realis dimension respectively; while illocutionary force and evidentiality are more sentential in nature, scoping over the first category of clausal operators and applying only to main clauses which are immediately dominated by a sentence node.

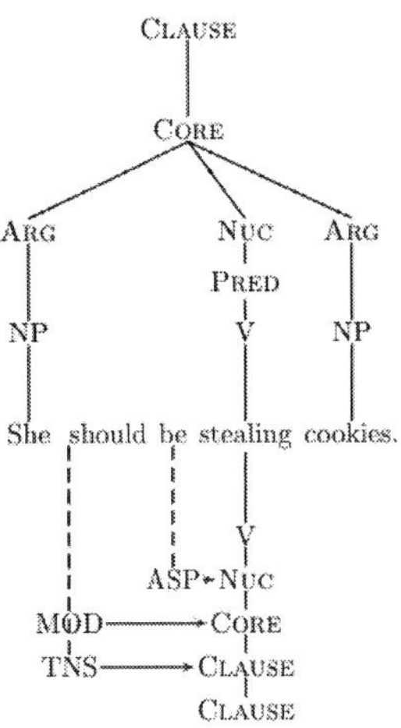

Figure 1: English clause structure with operator projection

An English clause with three grammatical operators is shown in Figure 1. The syntactic and the operator structures are projected above and below the sentence respectively. The aspectual operator expressed by the *be V-ing* construction applies to the nucleus. The deontic modal operator expressed by the *should* auxiliary applies to the core. The tense operator is expressed by the finite auxiliary *should.*

2.2 Semantic modifiers

The clause, core, and nucleus each have their own periphery, containing modifiers that combine with the non-peripheral constituent in that layer. Modifiers include prepositional phrases and adverbs. Just as the layer of application for each type of grammatical operator is semantically motivated, so too is the layer of application for each semantic category of modifier. Aspectual adverbs (e.g. *completely* or *continuously*) modify the nucleus and occur in the nuclear periphery; pace adverbs (e.g. *quickly*), manner adverbs (e.g. *carefully*) and temporal and locative modifiers (e.g. *yesterday, on Friday, in the kitchen, in an hour*) modify the core and occur in the core periphery, and epistemic and evidential adverbs (e.g. *evidently, probably*) modify the clause and occur in the clause periphery. The layering of modification also captures restrictions on the possible orderings for modifiers: if a modifier applies at a higher layer than another modifier, it cannot occur between that lower modifier and the verb. For example in (1c), but not in in (1a-b), the core modifier ***on Friday*** intervenes between the nucleus *destroyed* and the nuclear modifier ***completely***, and so the sentence is anomalous.

(1) a. Jane *destroyed* the painting **completely**$_{NUCMOD}$ **on Friday**$_{COREMOD}$.
b. Jane **completely**$_{NUCMOD}$ *destroyed* the painting **on Friday**$_{COREMOD}$.
c. # Jane *destroyed* the painting **on Friday**$_{COREMOD}$ **completely**$_{NUCMOD}$.

The application of operators and modifiers is also relevant when considering the structure of complex sentences with multiple predicates. This is discussed further in Section 2.3.

2.3 The structure and interpretation of complex event descriptions

While simple sentences are built around a single predicating element, with a single nucleus, core, clause and sentence, more complex sentences can contain multiple predicating elements, requiring a more complex syntactic structure to combine them. Traditional theories of grammar typically assume that syntactic units are either joined together via **coordination** inside a larger unit, or via **subordination** (with one unit embedded in the other, as either an argument or a modifier). RRG recognizes a third possible nexus type, **cosubordination**, which shares some properties with coordination, and some with subordination.

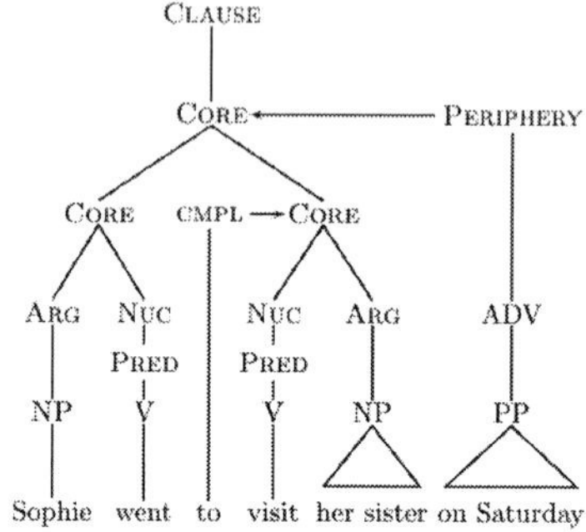

Figure 2: Core cosubordination

In cosubordination (Figure 2), two units of the same type are joined together to form a unit of that same type (i.e. two nuclei form a nucleus, two cores form a core, or two clauses form a clause). The operators and periphery (modifiers) that apply to that type are shared across both units (only the mother unit, and not the daughter units, has its own periphery and operators). In coordination, each unit has its own operators and periphery, and the two units join together to form a larger unit (e.g. two cores form a clause, two clauses form a sentence). A sentence instantiating core coordination is shown in Figure 3. In non-subordinate core junctures, each core has its own argument structure, but an argument can be shared between the two cores via a control or raising relationship (argument sharing is obligatory in core cosubordinations, and possible but not obligatory in core coordinations). In this case, the argument NP *Sophie* occurs in the first core, but is also an argument of the second core (the Actor in the visiting event).

The possible linkage relations (juncture-nexus types) can be arranged hierarchically in terms of the strength of the syntactic bond between the units: from closer to being integrated into a single unit (e.g. a complex predicate - nuclear cosubordination), to closer to being two separate units (e.g. sentential coordination). Nuclear junctures are the most compact, followed by core, clausal and sentential. Within each layer, cosubordination is the tightest nexus type, followed by subordination and then coordination. The hierarchy of syntactic relations aligns with a hierarchy of semantic relations according to the degree of semantic cohesion between the the two units: closer to being conceptualized as facets of a single event/action, or to being conceptualized as two distinct events/actions.

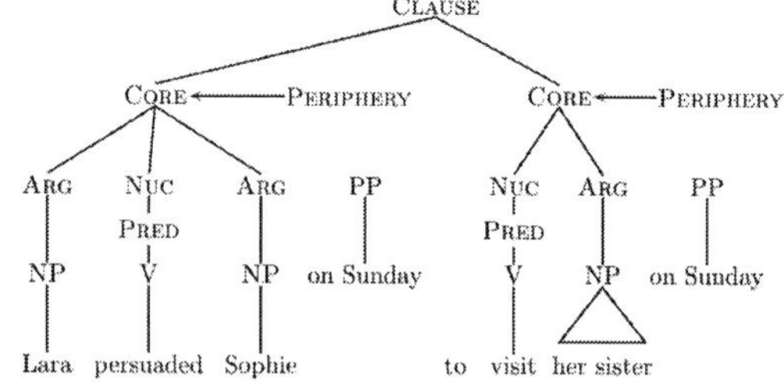

Figure 3: Core coordination

A cross-linguistically applicable breakpoint in the hierarchy of linkage relations was identified by Bohnemeyer and Van Valin (2017): constructions which combine two units using a core cosubordination linkage (or tighter) have the property of construing the described event as a single conceptual event, while constructions which combine two units using a core coordination linkage (or weaker) have the property of construing the described event as consisting of multiple conceptual events. The Macro Event Property

(MEP) (Bohnemeyer et al., 2007) is a possible semantic property of a syntactic construction (containing an event description). Constructions which have the MEP package an event representation such that any time-positional modifiers necessarily have scope over all of the subevents in the construction: the event is construed as more like a single event. Constructions which lack the MEP package an event representation such that multiple time-positional modifiers are possible (such that they each have scope over a different subpart of the complex event): the complex event is construed more like multiple events. (2) exemplifies this property using English infinitival constructions.

(2) a. Lara persuaded Sophie on Thursday to visit her sister on Saturday. *(Core coordination)*
b. Sophie went (#yesterday) to visit her sister today. *(Core cosubordination)*

Nuclear junctures necessarily have the MEP, as do cosubordinate core junctures, while core coordination, core subordination, and all clausal and sentential junctures lack the MEP. This fits neatly with the idea of a shared periphery: because time-positional modifiers occur in the core periphery, and core cosubordinations (as well as all nuclear junctures) share a single core periphery, time-positional modifiers necessarily have scope over the entire complex event. This distinction between complex events descriptions that have the MEP, construing the event as a single *macro event*, and those that lack the MEP, and construe the complex event as multiple *macro events*, is exploited in the semantic representation of the implemented grammar (see Section 4.3.1).

3 A typed feature structure approach to Construction Grammar

The term Construction Grammar describes a family of grammatical theories in which constructions (defined as form-meaning pairings) are basic units. Sign-based Construction Grammar (SBCG) (Sag, 2012) combines insights from HPSG (Pollard and Sag, 1994) and Berkeley Construction Grammar (Fillmore and Kay, 1996). The grammar signature is an inheritance hierarchy of types. Each type has an associated set of features, and the value of each feature is itself typed. Features and their type constraints are inherited in the type hierarchy: subtypes must have all the features and value type restrictions of their ancestors, plus any additional restrictions introduced for that subtype. Words and phrases are **signs** (pairings of form and meaning). Local trees are encoded as feature structures as shown in (3).

(3) $\begin{bmatrix} \text{MOTHER} & np \\ \text{DTRS} & \langle det, n \rangle \end{bmatrix}$

Although the proposed constraint-based RRG variant shares with SBCG the use of Frame Semantics (Fillmore, 1982), frames are embedded hierarchically rather than as a flat list. The focus of the present work is on the structure of complex event representations (distinguishing event frames, macroevents and propositions), rather than on the ability to handle phenomena such as quantifier scope ambiguity.[1]

4 A constraint-based variant of Role and Reference Grammar

Role and Reference Grammar (Van Valin, 2005) traditionally recognizes constructions as an important part of the grammar, but restricts them to cover only the more idiosyncratic structures in a language. Unlike constructions in SBCG and other unification-based construction grammars, RRG's constructions rely heavily on additional linking rules and template selection principles (Van Valin, 2005, p.244). RRG posits an inventory of abstract syntactic templates and linking relations (juncture-nexus types) which are distinct from grammatical construction types: these templates/relations may appear on the syntactic side of a constructional schema. Unlike standard RRG, where only idiosyncratic phenomena are captured with explicit constructional schemas, in the proposed constraint-based RRG variant all syntactic structures are captured as constructions (of varying degrees of abstraction).

[1] A flatter structure closer to Minimal Recursion Semantics (Copestake et al., 2005) may be considered in the future.

The various layers (nucleus, core, clause, sentence) are represented as subtypes of *layer*, a subtype of *sign* (Figure 4a). Other layer subtypes are *pp* (prepositional phrase) and *np* (noun phrase). As in SBCG, phrasal constructions (Figure 4b) are represented as feature structures with MOTHER and DTRS features.

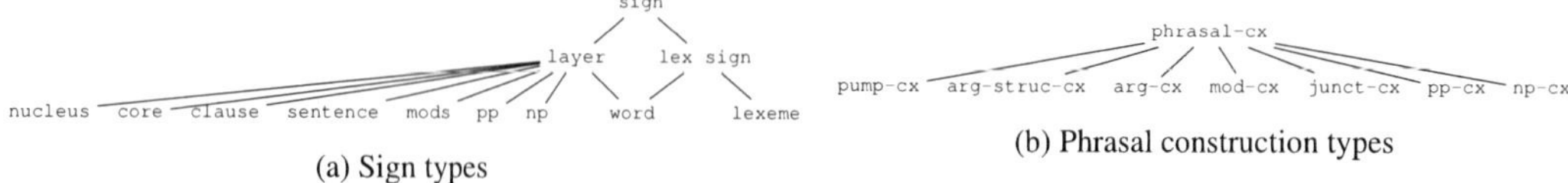

(a) Sign types

(b) Phrasal construction types

Figure 4: Type hierarchies in a constraint-based variant of RRG

The type signature for *sign* is shown in (4): objects of type *sign* have a SYN feature of type *syn-obj*,[2] and a SEM feature of type *sem-obj*. The subtype *layer* additionally introduces the boolean feature PERIPHERY, to indicate whether any peripheral modification has already been applied to that layer (cosubordination constructions require that the daughter layers have not yet had modification applied).

(4) $\begin{bmatrix} \textit{sign} & \\ \text{SYN} & \textit{syn-obj} \\ \text{SEM} & \textit{sem-obj} \end{bmatrix}$

(5) $\begin{bmatrix} \textit{layer} (\uparrow \textit{sign}) & \\ \text{PERIPHERY} & \textit{boolean} \end{bmatrix}$

(6) $\begin{bmatrix} \textit{pumping-cx} (\uparrow \textit{phrasal-cx}) & \\ \text{MOTHER} & \begin{bmatrix} \textit{layer} & \\ \text{SYN} & \boxed{1} \end{bmatrix} \\ \text{DTRS} & \left\langle \begin{bmatrix} \textit{layer} & \\ \text{SYN} & \boxed{1} \begin{bmatrix} \text{CLM} & \textit{clm-none} \end{bmatrix} \end{bmatrix} \right\rangle \end{bmatrix}$

Pumping constructions pass each non-complex layer up to the next layer. DTRS in a pumping construction is a singleton list containing one *layer* type (e.g. a *core*), and the MOTHER is the *layer* above (e.g. a *clause*). Syntactic (SYN) features are passed from the daughter to the mother, while some elements of the semantics (SEM) are changed from layer to layer (discussed in Section 4.3). The transition from nucleus to core is not captured in a pumping construction, but in an argument structure construction, as changes must be made to the valence list (SYN|VAL) (SYN values remain constant for all other layer transitions). Instead of RRG's standard linking algorithms, **argument structure constructions** assign the appropriate number and ordering of arguments positions to a core, and **argument constructions** add appropriate arguments to those positions.[3]

Figure 5 shows the derivation of a simple intransitive sentence (*Pat laughed*). A sentence is produced from a clause through a pumping construction (or via a more complex juncture). A minimum of four pumping constructions (or more complex juncture constructions) plus an argument construction are required to produce a sentence from a verb. As a consequence, there is a core node for every argument, unlike standard RRG. This tree structure captures more of the argument linking process than a standard RRG tree, where the linking algorithm is represented separately.

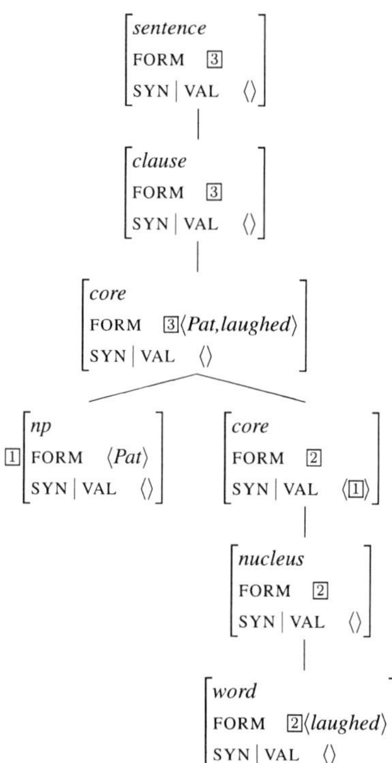

Figure 5: Simplified derivation *Pat laughed*

Juncture constructions combine two units of the same layer in coordinate or cosubordinate nexus. For example, a core cosubordination construction combines two daughter cores and produces a mother core, while a core coordination construction combines two daughter cores and produces a mother clause. Juncture constructions may place both syntactic (e.g. verb form, presence of a particular clause linkage

[2] I omit further discussion of the *syn-obj* type here for space reasons.

[3] This is English-centric, and may be adjusted in the future to allow for broader typological coverage.

marker) and semantic (e.g. subtypes of a certain semantic event frame) restrictions on their constituents.

4.1 Operators and modifiers

The *sem-obj* type (7) has a feature OPERATORS (OPS), which records the value of each of the nuclear, core and clausal operators that have been incorporated into a representation. These operators are then passed to the representation of the relevant semantic unit (see Section 4.3.1) at the time it is generated. In this way, the grammar is able to handle operators that occur on the surface between elements of a lower layer in the LSC (e.g. clausal operators inside the core, or tense morphemes attached to predicates).

Modifier constructions combine a layer in the LSC with something in its periphery. As discussed in Section 2.2, different semantic categories of verbal modifier apply to different layers in the clause. This restriction is captured by having a different modifier construction for each semantic category of modification, and restricting each modifier construction to apply to a particular layer (nucleus, core, clause or sentence). As modifiers combine a layer in the LSC with something in its periphery, all modifier constructions constrain the mother's PERIPHERY to $+$. This value is effectively reset each time a new layer is reached, as it is not passed from daughter to mother. While this approach does not allow for modifiers applicable to one layer to be interspersed between the elements of a lower layer, this could be improved in the future by adjusting the representation of modifiers to be more like the operator representation.

4.2 Comparison to a Tree Adjoining Grammar-based RRG formalization

The TAG-inspired approach to RRG formalization pursued by Osswald and Kallmeyer (2018) produces trees that are more consistent with standard RRG that the approach I have proposed. In the TAG approach, the trees are flatter, represent the fully derived structure rather than the steps involved in derivation, and capture the extended domain of locality in a way that is more consistent with standard RRG: long distance dependencies are captured using a 'wrapping substitution' mechanism, in which the predicate-argument structure that is the source of the long distance dependency is wrapped around the intervening elements. In the present approach, long distance dependencies would need to be percolated through the layered structure of the clause, as in Pollard and Sag (1994).

4.3 Semantics representation

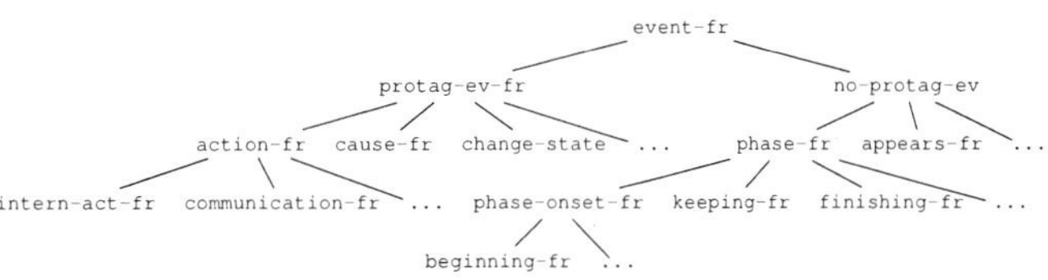

Figure 6: A section of the event frame type hierarchy

Although not explicitly arranged hierarchically, or using typed feature structures, the verbal representations in standard RRG can be straightforwardly adapted to hierarchically organized feature structure representations (*semantic frames*). RRG's lexical decomposition semantics already organizes verbs into a number of classes. A fragment of the proposed event frame hierarchy is shown in Figure 6. Each event frame is associated with a set of boolean aspectual features (STATIC, DYNAMIC, TELIC and PUNCTUAL), following Van Valin (2005). These features are used to restrict the application of constructions that are sensitive to the aspectual properties of their constituents, such as phase constructions (e.g. *begin to X*) and duration (e.g. *for an hour*) or time-to-completion modifiers (e.g. *in two hours*). Participant roles are already hierarchically organized in RRG, so that most roles are fairly specific but can also be categorized into more coarsely grained thematic relations and macro roles (see Van Valin, 2005, p.54). Verbs describing *activities* are represented with **do'** in the logical representation. This could be transformed into an abstract ACTOR role in an event frame, to be realized as EATER, RUNNER, TALKER and so on in specific event frames.

4.3.1 Semantic representation: entities, event frames, macroevents and propositions

Extending the idea of the Macro Event Property (Bohnemeyer et al., 2007; Bohnemeyer and Van Valin, 2017), a distinction is made between event frames, macroevents, and propositions. Macroevents are composed from the event frame in the nucleus, any additional event frame contributed by the argument structure construction, and any core cosubordination junctures. As the macroevent is built up from the nucleus to the core to be passed on to the clause, it is represented in SEM|FRAMES|BUILD-MACROEVENT (abbreviated to SEM|FRMS|B-MACRO). Once a core becomes a clause, either through a pumping construction (10), or through a core coordination construction, the *macro-event-obj* in BUILD-MACROEVENT is transferred to the MACRO-EVENTS (M-EVS) list in the first *proposition-obj* in the PROPOSITIONS (PROPS) list. The type signatures for *sem-obj*, *macro-event-obj* and *proposition-obj* are shown in (7-9):

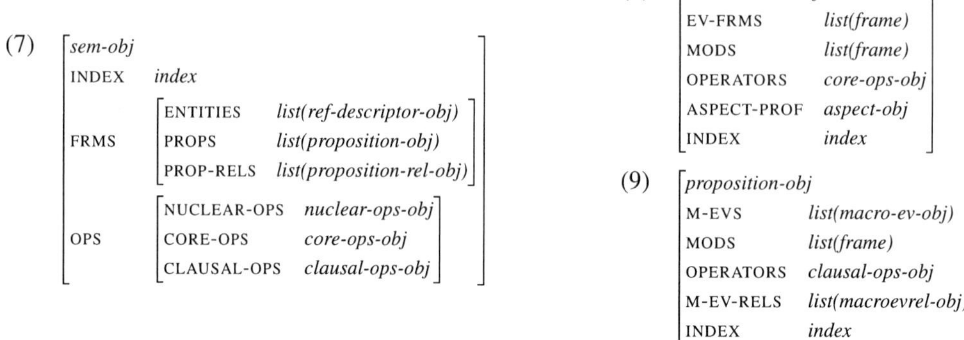

$list(\tau)$ represents a list containing only elements of type τ. Propositions (9) are composed from the macroevent/s contributed by the core/s that feed into a sentence. Core coordination constructions produce two macroevents, while core cosubordination constructions produce only one: the events contributed by each daughter core are integrated into the semantics of a single macroevent in the juncture construction.

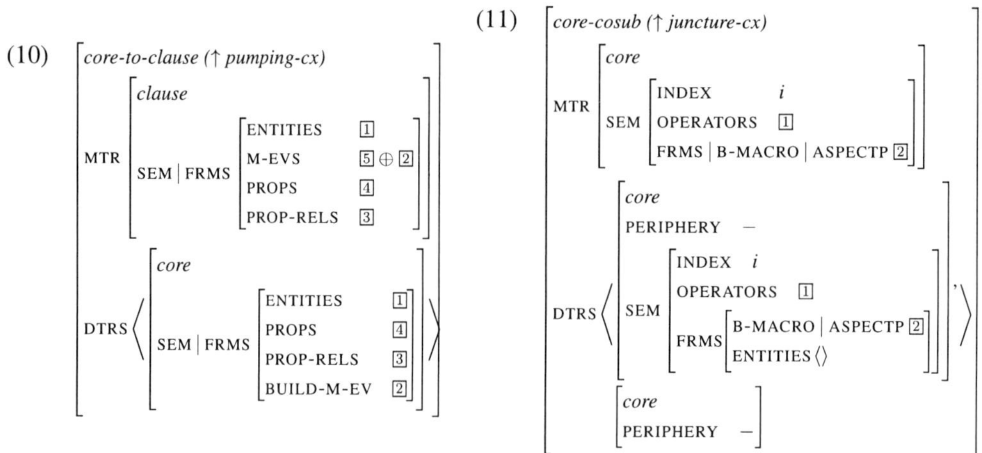

The precise relationship between event frames (contributed either by a predicate or by a construction) is specified in the constraints of each construction. Core layer modifiers are added to the MODS list of the *macro-event-obj*. The onset-phase construction shown in (12) specifies that the first core must contribute a *phase-onset-fr*, while the second core must contribute an *event-fr* which fills the EVENT role of the *phase-onset-fr*. The ultimate semantic output of a sentence is a list of entities, and a list of propositions (plus proposition relations, in the case of sentences containing multiple clause nodes).

(12) [*ccosub-onset-phase* (↑ *core-cosub*)
MTR [SEM | FRMS | B-MACRO | EV-FS ⟨ [3] [*phase-onset-fr* EVENT [4]] ⟩]
DTRS ⟨ [SEM | FRMS | B-MACRO | EV-FS ⟨[3]⟩], [SEM | FRMS | B-MACRO | EV-FS ⟨[4] *event-fr*⟩] ⟩]

5 Implementation in ALE

The Attribute Logic Engine (ALE) is a freeware logic programming and grammar parsing and generation system written in Prolog. For a full description of ALE, see Carpenter and Penn (2001). The proposed constraint-based RRG-variant is implemented for a fragment of English.[4] The current fragment contains a restricted set of 419 lexical items and 45 leaf node constructions. A semi-automatic expansion of the lexicon using FrameNet is planned. The implementation includes: a type-hierarchy, containing all types and their features; a list of constraints on types; a lexicon; a list of lexical rules; a list of phrase rules which map constituents to the daughters of a compatible construction, thus generating a mother constituent; a list of declarative statements which constrain the parser so that only the leaf construction types in the hierarchy (and not the more abstract parent types) can be parsed; and macros to simplify repeated chunks of code. Listing 1 shows the implementation of the constraints on the abstract *core-cosubordination construction* (11). Listing 2 shows the output of the `recsem()` command, which parses a sentence and displays the semantic output of a sentence: a list of entities and a list of propositions.

Listing 1: Core cosubordination constraints in ALE

```
coreCosub cons
   (mother:(core,
      syn:(category: Cat,
         clmm: clm_none),
      sem:(index:I,
         operators: 0,
         frames:(buildMacroEvent:(aspectprofile:Asp)))),
   dtrs:[(core,
        periphery: minus,
        syn:(category: Cat,
           clmm:clm_none),
        sem:(index:I,
           operators: 0,
           frames:(buildMacroEvent:(aspectprofile:Asp),
                 entities:      []))),
        (core, periphery: minus)]).
```

Listing 2: Semantic output for *The cat began to purr.*

```
sem_output
ENTS     referentdescriptor
         BOUNDED plus
         CAT cat_fr
            ENTITY [0]
         DEF definite
         IX [0]
         NUMBER sg
PROPS    proposition
         MACROEVS     macroEvent
                      ASPECTPROF [1] achievement
                      EV-FRMS beginning_fr
                         ASPECT [1]
                         PHASE_EV purring_fr
                            PROTAG [0]
                         SIT [2]
         OPERATORS    clauseops
                      TENSE past
         PROP_INDEX [2]
```

Constructions are parsed via phrase rules. Phrase rules in ALE specify an output, one or more constituents (`cat>`) in the order they must be encountered, and goals (`goal>`) which evaluate Prolog predicates with respect to variables from the output or constituents of the phrase rule. In this implementation, the type of each constituent is always *phrasal-cx*, and `cat>` is only ever sensitive to the constituent's MOTHER value. The phrase rule output is also a construction, and each item in its DTRS list must unify with the MOTHER of a particular constituent. The possible output construction types are restricted via the `goal`: only construction types which satisfy a specified Prolog predicate (defined in a list of declarative statements) are eligible. In this way, parsing is restricted to only leaf node construction types, and not their more abstract/underspecified supertypes.

6 Future work

The current implementation of this constraint-based variant of RRG has focused primarily on: a) building out the backbone of the layered structure of the clause; and b) the structure and semantic representation of complex event descriptions. Two major additional features are currently being developed: the incorporation of information structure (the third projection in RRG's LSC model), which will extend the model beyond parsing declarative sentences with broad focus; and aspectual coercion (c.f. Michaelis, 2004), which will increase the flexibility of the grammar in parsing event descriptions that do not make use of the default aspectual profile of a particular event.

[4]The full code plus user manual are available on Github: https://github.com/ebellingham/constraint-based-rrg

References

Bohnemeyer, J., N. J. Enfield, J. Essegbey, I. Ibarretxe-Antunano, S. Kita, F. Lüpke, and F. K. Ameka (2007). Principles of event segmentation in language: The case of motion events. *Language 83*(3), 495–532.

Bohnemeyer, J. and R. D. Van Valin (2017). The macro-event property and the layered structure of the clause. *Studies in Language 41*(1), 142–197.

Carpenter, B. (1992). *The Logic of Typed Feature Structures*. New York, NY, USA: Cambridge University Press.

Carpenter, B. and G. Penn (2001). *ALE: The attribute logic engine user's guide [Version 3.2.1]*. Carnegie-Mellon University.

Copestake, A., D. Flickinger, C. Pollard, and I. A. Sag (2005). Minimal Recursion Semantics: An Introduction. *Research on Language and Computation 3*(2-3), 281–332.

Fillmore, C. J. (1982). Frame Semantics. In *Linguistics in the Morning Calm*, pp. 111–137. Hanshin Publishing Co.

Fillmore, C. J. and P. Kay (1996). Construction grammar coursebook.

Foley, W. and R. D. Van Valin (1984). *Functional syntax and universal grammar*. Cambridge: Cambridge University Press.

Joshi, A. K. and Y. Schabes (1997). Tree-adjoining grammars. In *Handbook of formal languages*, pp. 69–123. Springer.

Kallmeyer, L. and R. Osswald (2017). Combining predicate-argument structure and operator projection: Clause structure in role and reference grammar. In *Proceedings of the 13th International Workshop on Tree Adjoining Grammars and Related Formalisms*, pp. 61–70.

Kallmeyer, L., R. Osswald, and R. D. Van Valin (2013). Tree wrapping for role and reference grammar. In *Formal Grammar*, pp. 175–190. Springer.

Michaelis, L. A. (2004). Type shifting in construction grammar: An integrated approach to aspectual coercion. *Cognitive Linguistics 15*(1), 1–67.

Osswald, R. and L. Kallmeyer (2018). Towards a formalization of role and reference grammar. In R. Kailuweit, L. Knkel, and E. Staudinger (Eds.), *Applying and Expanding Role and Reference Grammar*, NIHIN Studies, pp. 355–378. Freiburg: Albert-Ludwigs-Universität, Universitätsbibliothek.

Pollard, C. and I. A. Sag (1994). *Head-driven phrase structure grammar*. University of Chicago Press.

Sag, I. A. (2012). Sign-based construction grammar: An informal synopsis. In *Sign-based construction grammar*, Volume 193, pp. 69–202. CSLI: CSLI Publications.

Van Valin, R. D. (2005). *Exploring the syntax-semantics interface*. Cambridge: Cambridge University Press.

Van Valin, R. D. and R. J. LaPolla (1997). *Syntax*. Cambridge: Cambridge University Press.

Computational Syntax-Semantics Interface with Type-Theory of Acyclic Recursion for Underspecified Semantics

Roussanka Loukanova
Stockholm University
loukanova@gmail.com

Abstract

The paper provides a technique for algorithmic syntax-semantics interface in computational grammar with underspecified semantic representations of human language. The technique is introduced for expressions that contain NP quantifiers, by using computational, generalised Constraint-Based Lexicalised Grammar (GCBLG) that represents major, common syntactic characteristics of a variety of approaches to formal grammar and natural language processing (NLP). Our solution can be realised by any of the grammar formalisms in the CBLG class, e.g., Head-Driven Phrase Structure Grammar (HPSG), Lexical Functional Grammar (LFG), Categorial Grammar (CG). The type-theory of acyclic recursion L^{λ}_{ar}, provides facility for representing major semantic ambiguities, as underspecification, at the object level of the formal language of L^{λ}_{ar}, without recourse of meta-language variables. Specific semantic representations can be obtained by instantiations of underspecified L^{λ}_{ar}-terms, in context. These are subject to constraints provided by a newly introduced feature-structure description of syntax-semantics interface in GCBLG.

1 Introduction

Ambiguity permeates human language, in all of its manifestations, by interdependences, across lexicon, syntax, semantics, discourse, context, etc. Alternative interpretations may persist even when specific context and discourse resolve or discard some specific instances in syntax and semantics. We present computational grammar that integrates lexicon, syntax, types, constraints, and semantics. The formal facilities of the grammar have components that integrate syntactic constructions with semantic representations. The syntax-semantic interface, internally in the grammar, handles some ambiguities as phenomena of underspecification in human language.

We employ a computational grammar, which we call Generalised Constraint-Based Lexicalised Grammar (GCBLG). The formal system GCBLG uses feature-value descriptions and constraints in a grammar with a hierarchy of dependent types, which covers lexicon, phrasal structures, and semantic representations. In GCBLG, for the syntax, we use feature-value descriptions, similar to that in Sag et al. (2003), which are presented formally in Loukanova (2017a) as a class of formal languages designating mathematical structures of functional domains of linguistics information. GCBLG is a generalisation from major lexical and syntactic facilities of frameworks in the class of Constraint-Based Lexicalist Grammar (CBLG) approaches. To some extend, this is reminiscence of Vijay-Shanker and Weir (1994). We lift the idea of extending classic formal grammars to cover semantic representations with semantic underspecification via syntax-semantics interface within computational grammar.

We introduce the technique here for varieties of grammar formalisms from the CBLG approach, in particular: Categorial Grammar (CG), e.g., see Moortgat (1996); Head-Driven Phrase Structure Grammar (HPSG), e.g., see Pollard and Sag (1994); Lexical Functional Grammar (LFG), e.g., see Bresnan (2001), Dalrymple (2001), Kroeger (2004); Tree-Adjoining Grammar (TAG), e.g., see Joshi et al. (1975); Joshi (1987); and other grammar approaches, such as the Grammatical Framework GF, see Ranta (2011). The valance features that we use here with corresponding semantic representations can be translated directly into HPSG, LFG, and Categorial Grammar (CG).

Proceedings of the IWCS 2019 Workshop on Computing Semantics with Types, Frames and Related Structures, pages 37–48
Gothenburg, Sweden, May 24, 2019.

The grammar rules and constraints in GCBLG, in syntax and lexicon, carry semantic representations. The formal language of the semantic representations is a specialised feature-value encoding of terms of the formal language of acyclic recursion $\mathrm{L}^{\lambda}_{\mathrm{ar}}$, see Moschovakis (2006).

2 Overview of Moschovakis Type-Theory of Acyclic Recursion

2.1 Syntax of L^{λ}_{ar}

$\mathsf{Types}_{\mathrm{L}^{\lambda}_{\mathrm{ar}}}$ is the smallest set defined recursively, e.g., by presenting the rules in Backus-Naur form:

$$\tau ::= \mathsf{e} \mid \mathsf{t} \mid \mathsf{s} \mid (\tau \to \tau) \qquad \text{(Types)}$$

Typed Vocabulary of $\mathrm{L}^{\lambda}_{\mathrm{ar}}$: For each type $\tau \in$ Types, $\mathrm{L}^{\lambda}_{\mathrm{ar}}$ has typed constants, and variables.
Constants K: a denumerable (e.g., finite) set, $K_\tau = \{\mathsf{c_0}^\tau, \dots, \mathsf{c}^\tau_k\}$, $K = \bigcup_\tau K_\tau$
Pure variables PV: a denumerable set: $\mathsf{PV}_\tau = \{\mathsf{v_0}, \mathsf{v_1}, \dots\}$; $\mathsf{PV} = \bigcup_\tau \mathsf{PV}_\tau$
Recursion (memory) variables RV: a denumerable set: $\mathsf{RV}_\tau = \{\mathsf{r_0}, \mathsf{r_1}, \dots\}$; $\mathsf{RV} = \bigcup_\tau \mathsf{RV}_\tau$
The sets of constants and variables of both kinds are mutually distinct: $K \neq \mathsf{RV} \neq \mathsf{PV}$.

Terms of $\mathrm{L}^{\lambda}_{\mathrm{ar}}$: The set of the terms of $\mathrm{L}^{\lambda}_{\mathrm{ar}}$ is $\mathsf{Terms} = \cup_{\tau \in \mathsf{Types}} \mathsf{Terms}_\tau$, where for every $\tau \in$ Types, the terms in Terms_τ are defined recursively as follows:

- *Constants*: If $\mathsf{c} \in K_\tau$, then $\mathsf{c} \in \mathsf{Terms}_\tau$, denoted by $c : \tau$ and c^τ
- *Variables*: If $x \in \mathsf{PV}_\tau \cup \mathsf{RV}_\tau$, then $x \in \mathsf{Terms}_\tau$, denoted by $x : \tau$ and x^τ
- *Application Terms*: If $A \in \mathsf{Terms}_{(\sigma\to\tau)}$ and $B \in \mathsf{Terms}_\sigma$, then $A(B) \in \mathsf{Terms}_\tau$, denoted by $A(B) : \tau$ and $[A(B)]^\tau$
- *λ-abstraction terms:* If $x \in \mathsf{PV}_\sigma$, and $A \in \mathsf{Terms}_\tau$, then $\lambda(x)(A) \in \mathsf{Terms}_{(\sigma\to\tau)}$, denoted by $\lambda(x)(A) : (\sigma \to \tau)$ and $[\lambda(x)(A)]^{(\sigma\to\tau)}$
- *Recursion terms:* For any $n \geq 0$, if $A_i \in \mathsf{Terms}_{\sigma_i}$ $(i = 0, \dots, n)$ and $p_i \in \mathsf{RV}_{\sigma_i}$ $(i = 1, \dots, n)$ are such that $p_1, \dots, p_n$ are pairwise different, and the sequence $\{\, p_1 := A_1, \dots, p_n := A_n \,\}$ satisfies the Acyclicity Constraint, i.e., it is *acyclic*, then A_0 where $\{p_1 := A_1, \dots, p_n := A_n\} \in \mathsf{Terms}_{\sigma_0}$. The type assignment of the recursion term is denoted by:

$$A_0 \ \mathsf{where} \ \{\, p_1 := A_1, \dots, p_n := A_n \,\} : \sigma_0 \qquad (1a)$$
$$[A_0 \ \mathsf{where} \ \{\, p_1 := A_1, \dots, p_n := A_n \,\}]^{\sigma_0} \qquad (1b)$$

Acyclicity Constraint (AC): the sequence of assignments $\{p_1 := A_1, \dots, p_n := A_n\}$ is *acyclic* iff there is a function $\mathsf{rank} : \{p_1, \dots, p_n\} \longrightarrow \mathbb{N}$ such that, for all $p_i, p_j \in \{p_1, \dots, p_n\}$,

$$\text{if } p_j \text{ occurs freely in } A_i \text{ then } \mathsf{rank}(p_j) < \mathsf{rank}(p_i) \qquad (2)$$

We use the meta-symbol $\equiv$ for identity between expressions, e.g., $E_1 \equiv E_2$, and in abbreviations.

The sets $\mathsf{FreeV}(A)$ and $\mathsf{BoundV}(A)$, respectively of the free and bound variables of a term A, are defined by structural recursion, in the usual way, with the exception of the recursion terms. For any given recursion term $A \equiv [A_0 \,\mathsf{where}\, \{p_1 := A_1, \dots, p_n := A_n\}]$, all occurrences of $p_1, \dots, p_n \in \mathsf{RV}$ in A are bound, and all other free (bound) occurrences of variables (constants) in $A_0, \dots, A_n$ are also free (bound) in A.

The reduction calculus of $\mathrm{L}^{\lambda}_{\mathrm{ar}}$ has a set of reduction rules that reduce each $\mathrm{L}^{\lambda}_{\mathrm{ar}}$-term A to its unique, up to congruence, canonical form $\mathsf{cf}(A)$, i.e., $A \Rightarrow \mathsf{cf}(A)$. Informally, for every $A, B \in$ Terms:

$A \approx B$ iff (1) A and B are proper terms and their denotations are equal and computed by the same algorithm determined by $\mathsf{cf}(A)$ and $\mathsf{cf}(B)$; (2) or, A and B are immediate, and A and B have the same denotations.

See Moschovakis (2006) and Loukanova (2016, 2019, 2018), for details on the denotational and algorithmic semantics of $\mathrm{L}^{\lambda}_{\mathrm{ar}}$. For the first representation of semantic underspecification with the theory of acyclic algorithms, see Loukanova (2007).

3 Underspecified Terms and Universal Syntax

Definition 1 (Underspecified $\mathrm{L}_{\mathrm{ar}}^{\lambda}$-Terms). *For any* $A \in \mathsf{Terms}$, *we call* A *an* underspecified term, *in case* $\mathsf{FreeV}(A) \cap \mathsf{RV} \neq \varnothing$, *i.e., when* A *has free occurrences of recursion variables; otherwise* A *is* specified.

We represent some of the semantic ambiguities of natural language sentences by rendering them into underspecified $\mathrm{L}_{\mathrm{ar}}^{\lambda}$-terms. In this paper, we consider a class of typical ambiguous sentences, which have different scope readings, due to occurrences of multiple quantifier NPs in them. For any such sentence Φ, direct representation of alternative readings, by a set of different $\mathrm{L}_{\mathrm{ar}}^{\lambda}$-terms, is available, e.g., $\Phi \xrightarrow{\mathsf{render}} A_i$, $i = 1, \ldots, n$, for some $n \geq 1$. Without any specific context, all of these alternative readings can be potentially viable. Instead of rendering Φ into the set of these specific terms, e.g., by some (syntactic or other) analyses, we render Φ into a single, underspecified term A that represents the set of the alternatives. When context information is available, e.g., by data driven methods, individual or all A_i can be derived from A. That can be done by instantiating the free recursion variables of A, and thus instantiating A, via expanding A by adding recursion assignments that bind its free recursion variables. We impose constraints over the free recursion variables $\mathsf{FreeV}(A) \cap \mathsf{RV}$, e.g., due to the syntactic structure of A, via syntax-semantic analysis, to prevent undesirable alternative instantiations and denotational interpretations $\mathsf{den}^{\mathfrak{A}}(A)(g)$.

Informally, we can restrict the instantiations of A by constraints over possible bindings of recursion variables that occur in A. For any given $A, R \in \mathsf{Terms}$ and $p \in \mathsf{RV}$, the relation $(R \ \mathsf{rBind}\ p)$ holds between R and p in A, when R *recursively binds* p in A, via a sequence of recursion assignments and/or by λ-abstraction across recursion assignments. Thus, rBind provides *specification relation* between underspecified and specified $\mathrm{L}_{\mathrm{ar}}^{\lambda}$-terms. The formal treatment of rBind, which is not in the subject of this paper, is based on the binding relation introduced in Loukanova (2017b). Here, we focus on the technique of rendering natural language expressions into underspecified terms, via syntax-semantics interface.

For example, the terms in (3d)–(3f) render the sentence "Fido barks", via unordered, i.e., abstract, universal syntax. (3c) renders the verb "barks", which is of lexical type *verb* in the lexicon, to the $\mathrm{L}_{\mathrm{ar}}^{\lambda}$-term T_b. T_b has in its where-assignment, the term $barks : (\widetilde{\mathsf{e}} \to \widetilde{t})$, which is not a constant, but a complex term that caries information about time in relation to possible, underspecified time of potential utterance, see Loukanova (2011b). While the term $T_b : \widetilde{t}$ is of sentential type, it is unsaturated because it has a free recursion variable p that fills the argument slot of b, and which is without any constraint over it, regarding possible binding of p.

- NP word in lexicon; semantically specified:

$$[\text{Fido}]_{\text{NP}} \xrightarrow{\mathsf{render}} T_i \equiv i \ \mathsf{where}\ \{\, i := \mathit{fido} \,\} : \widetilde{\mathsf{e}} \tag{3a}$$

- V lexeme in lexicon; rendered to a constant; semantically specified:

$$[\text{bark}]_{\text{V}} \xrightarrow{\mathsf{render}} T_{lex-b}^{(\widetilde{\mathsf{e}}\to\widetilde{t})} \equiv bark : (\widetilde{\mathsf{e}} \to \widetilde{t}) \tag{3b}$$

- Inflected V word in lexicon; semantically underspecified term carrying information about time; unsaturated for $p \in \mathsf{FreeV}(T_b^{\widetilde{t}})$; it becomes constrained VP in the sentence analysis:

$$[\text{barks}]_{\text{V}} \xrightarrow{\mathsf{render}} T_b^{\widetilde{t}} \equiv b(p) \ \mathsf{where}\ \{\, b := barks \,\} : \widetilde{t} \tag{3c}$$

- Sentence: universal, unordered syntax with SynSem; semantically underspecified; SynSem constrained:

$$\{\, [\text{Fido}]_{\text{NP}}, [\text{barks}]_{\text{VP}} \,\}_{\text{S}} \xrightarrow{\mathsf{render}} T_1 \equiv b(p) \ \mathsf{where}\ \{\, i := \mathit{fido},\ b := barks \,\} : \widetilde{t} \ \ \mathsf{such\ that}\ \{\, (i \ \mathsf{rBind}\ p) \,\} \tag{3d}$$

- Universal, unordered syntax with SynSem; semantically specified by the SynSem constraint:

$$\{\, [\text{Fido}]_{\text{NP}}, [\text{barks}]_{\text{VP}} \,\}_{\text{S}} \xrightarrow{\mathsf{render}} T_{\mathsf{univ}}^{1} \equiv b(p) \ \mathsf{where}\ \{\, p := i,\ i := \mathit{fido},\ b := barks \,\} \tag{3e}$$

- Semantically specified by the SynSem constraint; reduced chain assignments:

$$\{\, [\text{Fido}]_{\text{NP}}, [\text{barks}]_{\text{VP}} \,\}_{\text{S}} \xrightarrow{\mathsf{render}} T \equiv T_{\mathsf{univ}} \equiv b(p) \ \mathsf{where}\ \{\, p := \mathit{fido},\ b := barks \,\} \tag{3f}$$

- Surface ordered syntax with SynSem; semantically specified by the SynSem constraint:

$$\{\, [\text{Fido}]_{\text{NP}}, [\text{barks}]_{\text{VP}} \,\}_{\text{S}} \xrightarrow{\text{render}} T \equiv T_{\text{univ}} \equiv b(p) \text{ where } \{\, p := \mathit{fido},\ b := \mathit{barks} \,\} \tag{3g}$$

An alternative syntax-semantics analysis of the same sentence "Fido barks", can be obtained by using a λ-term $[T'_b]^{(\widetilde{\mathrm{e}} \to \widetilde{t})}$ rendering a VP like "barks", as in (4), the type of which, via $\lambda(x)$-abstraction, reflects that it is of a functional type. This analysis results in the same term for rendering the sentence, as in (3g), but with different intermediate reductions of the canonical forms. The analysis uses intermediate steps with γ^*-reduction, or, alternatively, γ-reduction, introduced in Loukanova (2019, 2018) for canonical forms cf_{γ^*} and cf_{γ}, correspondingly. These reduction extensions of the classic reduction from Moschovakis (2006), provide computational simplifications in many cases, like this one.

- Inflected V word of type *verb* in lexicon; $p' \in \mathsf{FreeV}(T'_b)$, $p'(x)$ designates an actant; semantically underspecified:

$$[\text{barks}]_{\text{VP}} \xrightarrow{\text{render}} [T'_b]^{(\widetilde{\mathrm{e}} \to \widetilde{t})} \equiv [\lambda(x)(b(p'(x))) \text{ where } \{\, b := \mathit{barks} \,\}] : (\widetilde{\mathrm{e}} \to \widetilde{t}) \tag{4}$$

In (5a)–(5e), we present stages of syntax-semantics analysis, of a sentence with one quantifier NP and an intransitive verb, via unordered, i.e., abstract, universal syntax-semantics interface. (5b) renders the verb "barks", which is of lexical type *verb* (a subtype of the type *word*) in the lexicon, to the $\mathrm{L}^{\lambda}_{\mathrm{ar}}$-term T_b. The term T_b has in its where-assignment, the term $\mathit{barks} : (\widetilde{\mathrm{e}} \to \widetilde{t})$, which is not a constant, but a complex term that caries information about time in relation to possible time of a potential utterance, see Loukanova (2011b). While the term $T_b : \widetilde{t}$ is of sentential type, it is unsaturated because it has a free recursion variable p that fills the argument slot of b, and which is without any constraint over it, regarding possible binding of p. The syntactic structure of the sentence saturates the syntactic argument of the VP, $[\text{barks}]_{\text{VP}}$, with the subject NP, e.g., $[\text{every dog}]_{\text{NP}}$.

- NP phrase, in grammar with SynSem; semantically specified:

$$\begin{aligned}[\text{Every, dog}]_{\text{NP}} &\xrightarrow{\text{render}} [K]^{((\widetilde{\mathrm{e}} \to \widetilde{\mathrm{t}}) \to \widetilde{\mathrm{t}})} \\ &\equiv [Q(d)]^{((\widetilde{\mathrm{e}} \to \widetilde{\mathrm{t}}) \to \widetilde{\mathrm{t}})} \text{ where } \{\, Q := \mathit{every},\ d := \mathit{dog} \,\}\end{aligned} \tag{5a}$$

- Inflected V word in lexicon; semantically underspecified term carrying information about time; unsaturated for $p \in \mathsf{FreeV}(T^{\widetilde{t}}_b)$; it becomes constrained VP in the sentence analysis:

$$[\text{barks}]_{\text{VP}} \xrightarrow{\text{render}} [T_b]^{\tilde{\mathrm{t}}} \equiv b(p) \text{ where } \{\, b^{(\tilde{\mathrm{e}} \to \tilde{\mathrm{t}})} := \mathit{barks}^{(\tilde{\mathrm{e}} \to \tilde{\mathrm{t}})} \,\} : \tilde{\mathrm{t}} \tag{5b}$$

- Sentence: universal, unordered syntax with SynSem; semantically underspecified; SynSem constrained:

$$\begin{aligned}\{\, [\text{Every dog}]_{\text{NP}}, [\text{barks}]_{\text{VP}} \,\}_{\text{S}} \xrightarrow{\text{render}} [T]^{\tilde{\mathrm{t}}} \equiv i \text{ where } \{ \\ k := Q(d),\ Q := \mathit{every},\ d := \mathit{dog}, \\ h := b(p),\ b := \mathit{barks} \,\} \\ \text{such that } \{\, (k \text{ rBind } p) \,\}\end{aligned} \tag{5c}$$

- Universal, unordered syntax with SynSem; semantically specified by SynSem constraint:

$$\begin{aligned}\xrightarrow{\text{process}} [T]^{\tilde{\mathrm{t}}} \equiv i \text{ where } \{\, i := k(\lambda(x)(h(x))) \approx k(h), \\ k := Q(d),\ Q := \mathit{every},\ d := \mathit{dog}, \\ h := \lambda(x)(b(p'(x))),\ p' := \lambda(x)(x),\ b := \mathit{barks} \,\} \\ \text{such that } \{\, (k \text{ rBind } p') \,\}\end{aligned} \tag{5d}$$

- Surface ordered syntax with SynSem; semantically specified by the SynSem constraint:

$$\begin{aligned}\{\, [\text{Every dog}]_{\text{NP}}\ [\text{barks}]_{\text{VP}} \,\}_{\text{S}} \xrightarrow{\text{render}} [T]^{\tilde{\mathrm{t}}} \equiv i \text{ where } \{\, i := k(\lambda(x)(h(x))) \approx k(h), \\ k := Q(d),\ Q := \mathit{every},\ d := \mathit{dog}, \\ h := \lambda(x)(b(p'(x))),\ p' := \lambda(x)(x),\ b := \mathit{barks} \,\} \\ \text{such that } \{\, (k \text{ rBind } p') \,\}\end{aligned} \tag{5e}$$

Note that the tree structures of the syntactic analyses in Sect. 6 have unordered daughters, and in essence, these are three demential graphs.

4 Syntax-Semantics Interface in GCBLG by the Type-Theory of Acyclic Recursion

A formal background on generalised GCBLG is given in Loukanova (2017a). We use a formal feature-value language for type-theoretical descriptions of computational syntax of human language. Sag et al. (2003) is a detailed introduction to formal grammar of human language, by providing and using theoretical linguistics. In this version of generalised GCBLG, semantic representations of human language expressions, are provided by $\mathrm{L}^{\lambda}_{\mathrm{ar}}$-terms of the formal language of acyclic recursion $\mathrm{L}^{\lambda}_{\mathrm{ar}}$, by using feature-value structures, via the technique introduced in Loukanova (2011a). Here, we provide two of the major grammatical rules of GCBLG, enhanced with semantic representation, and a new, additional feature-value description on constraints over semantic representations, via syntax-semantics interface. For this, we introduce a new feature SYNSEM of type *synsem*, with values of type *list-of(propositions)*.

The analysed natural language expressions are rendered into $\mathrm{L}^{\lambda}_{\mathrm{ar}}$-terms, in canonical forms, by using feature-value representations of the recursion terms, according to the following rule:

Rendering syntactic structures into $\mathrm{L}^{\lambda}_{\mathrm{ar}}$-terms: Assume that a natural language expression E is analysed by GCBLG as a feature-value description $F(A)$. Assume that, in $F(A)$, the value of the feature T-HEAD is a $\mathrm{L}^{\lambda}_{\mathrm{ar}}$-term A_0, and the value of the feature WHERE is a sequence $\overrightarrow{p} := \overrightarrow{A}$ of where-assignments. Then, $E \xrightarrow{\text{render}} A_0 \text{ where } \{ \overrightarrow{p} := \overrightarrow{A} \}$. The value of the feature L-TYPE is the $\mathrm{L}^{\lambda}_{\mathrm{ar}}$-type of A_0. We use recursion variables to designate the rendering terms in the feature-value descriptions, which can be used in the combined terms.

The rules HSR and HCR1 take as inputs expressions that have semantic representations in canonical forms and generate phrases with semantic representations that are in canonical forms too. The values of T-HEAD and WHERE of the left hand side of the rules are determined by: the semantic types T_1 and T_2 of the daughter nodes; the values of T-HEAD and WHERE in the daughters' feature structures on the right hand side; and the definition of the canonical form $\mathsf{cf}(A)$ of each term A.

Head Specifier Rule (HSR): (6)

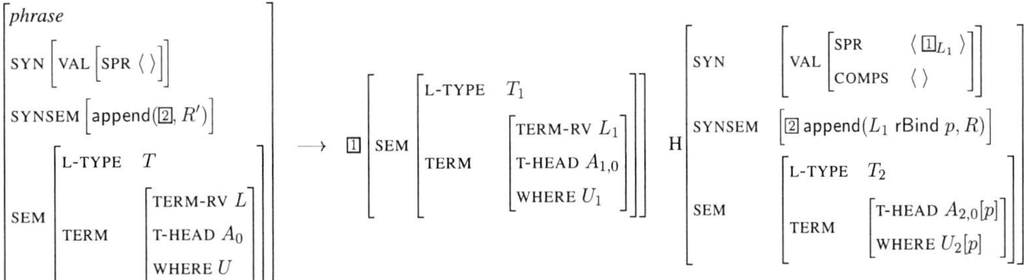

Head Complement Rule (HCR1): (7)

$$\begin{bmatrix} \textit{phrase} \\ \text{SYN}\ \left[\text{VAL}\ \left[\text{COMPS}\ \boxed{a}\right]\right] \\ \text{SYNSEM}\ \left[\mathsf{append}(\boxed{2}, R')\right] \\ \text{SEM}\ \begin{bmatrix} \text{L-TYPE} & T \\ \text{TERM} & \begin{bmatrix} \text{TERM-RV} & L \\ \text{T-HEAD} & A_0 \\ \text{WHERE} & U \end{bmatrix} \end{bmatrix} \end{bmatrix} \longrightarrow \text{H} \begin{bmatrix} \text{SYN}\ \left[\text{VAL}\ \left[\text{COMPS}\ \begin{bmatrix} \text{FIRST} & \boxed{1}_{L_1} \\ \text{REST} & \boxed{a}\,[\textit{list}] \end{bmatrix}\right]\right] \\ \text{SYNSEM}\ \left[\boxed{2}\,\mathsf{append}(L_1\ \mathsf{rBind}\ p, R)\right] \\ \text{SEM}\ \begin{bmatrix} \text{L-TYPE} & T_2 \\ \text{TERM} & \begin{bmatrix} \text{T-HEAD} & A_{2,0}[p] \\ \text{WHERE} & U_2[p] \end{bmatrix} \end{bmatrix} \end{bmatrix} \boxed{1} \left[\text{SEM}\ \begin{bmatrix} \text{L-TYPE} & T_1 \\ \text{TERM} & \begin{bmatrix} \text{TERM-RV} & L_1 \\ \text{T-HEAD} & A_{1,0} \\ \text{WHERE} & U_1 \end{bmatrix} \end{bmatrix}\right]$$

In both rules (6)–(7), $p \in \mathsf{RV}$, $A_{2,0}[p]$, $U_2[p]$ indicate that p may fill up some argument slots in some of the sub-terms, and the following cases can be realised:

Case1: $T_i \equiv (\sigma \to \tau)$ and $T_j \equiv \sigma$, for $i, j \in \{1, 2\}$ and $i \neq j$, $T \equiv \tau$

There are two sub-cases, (8) and (9), for the term $[A_0 \text{ where } U]$ in (6)–(7):

(1) if $A_{j,0}$ is immediate, then:

$$A_0 \equiv A_{i,0}(A_{j,0}) \text{ and } U \equiv \mathsf{append}(U_1, U_2) \tag{8}$$

(2) otherwise, i.e., if $A_{j,0}$ is proper, then:

$$A_0 \equiv A_{i,0}(q_0) \text{ and } U \equiv \mathsf{append}(\{q_0 := A_{j,0}\}, \mathsf{append}(U_1, U_2)) \tag{9}$$

Case2: $T_2 : \tilde{\mathrm{t}}$; and $T_1 : ((\tilde{\mathrm{e}} \to \tilde{\mathrm{t}}) \to \tilde{\mathrm{t}})$ or $T_1 : ((\tilde{\mathrm{e}} \to \tilde{\mathrm{t}}) \to ((\tilde{\mathrm{e}} \to \tilde{\mathrm{t}}) \to \tilde{\mathrm{t}}))$

The binding constraints in the value of the feature SYNSEM provide suitable terms for A_0 and U, by combining the parts $A_{j,0}, U_j$, for $j = 1, 2$, and adding new constraints, as needed. The detailed specifications use the definition of the relation rBind.

Case2 covers expressions such as NPs, VPs, and sentences S, where some argument slots are bound by sub-terms of the renderings of NP quantifiers, via recursion variables. The technique is exemplified by the analysis of the sentence "Every cat hugs some dog", which represents a general pattern for multiple quantifier scopes. It is presented in Fig. 3.

5 Scope Underspecification and Specification

Scope Underspecification: The feature-value structural description given in Fig. 3 is a pattern of one of the possible ways to represent multiple semantic scopes of quantification. The syntax-semantics interface is provided by the HSR and HCR1 rules of GCBLG, while the formal calculi of $\mathrm{L}^{\lambda}_{\mathrm{ar}}$, provides terms for algorithmic semantics. A sentence that has occurrences of multiple quantifier NPs can be rendered into a single $\mathrm{L}^{\lambda}_{\mathrm{ar}}$-term that represents the multiple possibilities simultaneously. It is underspecified, by having constrained free recursion variables filling up the argument slots that are bound by the corresponding NPs.

Scope Specification: The binding relation rBind in $\mathrm{L}^{\lambda}_{\mathrm{ar}}$ provides a syntax-semantics facility to constrain the possible bindings in specific scopes, via restricting free recursion variables occurring in an underspecified term. An underspecified term can be expanded into specified terms only if they satisfy the rBind-constraints. Thus, constraints expressed by rBind also restrict the possible interpretations of the free recursion variables. For instance, the semantic rendering in Fig. 3 can be expanded into specified semantic representation, which has to satisfy the constraints imposed by the structural combinations. Fig. (4) presents one of the available possibilities to instantiate the free recursion variables, i.e., to bind them by the corresponding NP quantifiers.

6 Grammar Analyses with Syntax-Semantics Interface in GCBLG

In this section, we provide several analyses of typical sentences with head verbs taking NPs as their syntactic, and corresponding semantic, arguments. We exemplify the classes of intransitive and transitive head verbs having NP subjects and single NP complements.

Note that in the analysis in Fig. 1, we do not render the NP that is a proper name into a term of a generalised quantifier, since that would introduce unnecessary complexity in the analysis of expressions of this kind. Furthermore, the term $[T_b]^{\tilde{\mathrm{t}}}$ that renders the VP is as in (5b). Optionally, we can use a λ-abstraction term $[T'_b]^{(\tilde{\mathrm{e}} \to \tilde{t})}$, and then, the sentence gets rendered to an algorithmically equivalent term by the γ^*-reduction calculus of $\mathrm{L}^{\lambda}_{\mathrm{ar}}$, see Loukanova (2019, 2018).

In Fig. 2, we present a syntax-semantics analysis of a sentence with a single quantifier NP, in the subject position of the intransitive V. Optionally, we can use a λ-abstraction term $[T'_b]^{(\tilde{\mathrm{e}} \to \tilde{t})}$, resulting in an algorithmically equivalent term for the sentence, by the γ^*-reduction calculus of $\mathrm{L}^{\lambda}_{\mathrm{ar}}$.

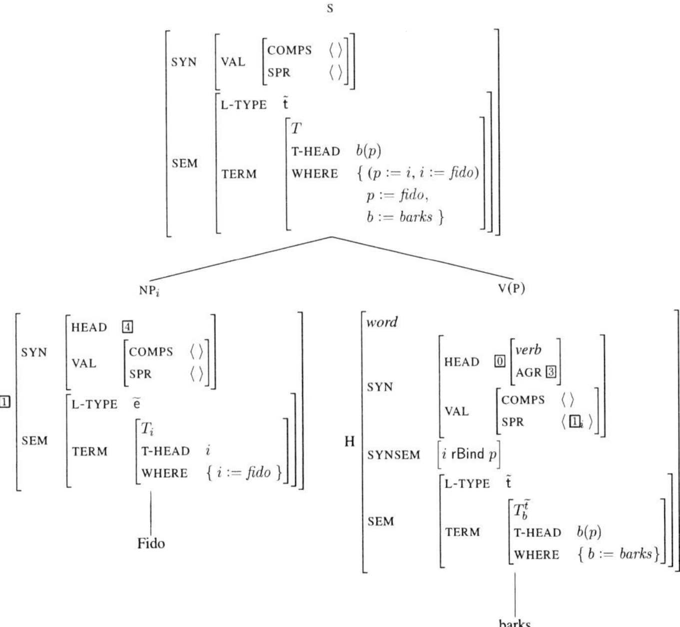

Figure 1: A Proper Name as the Specifier of an Intransitive Verb

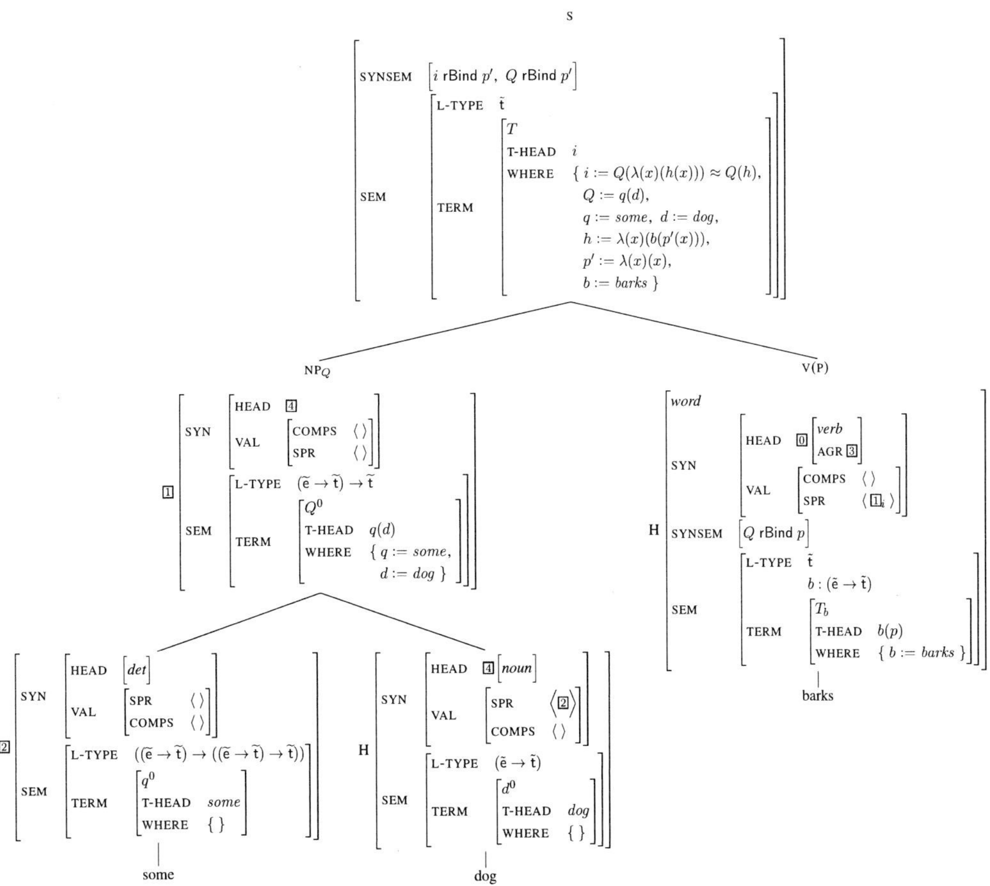

Figure 2: Quantifier NP in Subject Position, Specified

In Fig. 3, we present a syntax-semantics analysis of a sentence with two quantifier NPs, in subject and compliment positions of the head verb V. In Fig. 4, we present its specification to one of the alternative scope distributions. In it, we have specified the VP at the intermediate level of the analysis, in the node marked by (n_1) VP. Pragmatically, it is more viable for this node to be underspecified as it is in 3, and the specification is at the node (n_0) S, at the sentence level, e.g., when disambiguating information is available at that level.

In Fig. 5, we present an optional analysis of the same sentence, by rendering the head verb to a λ-term, which is congruent to $\lambda(x_{d_2})\lambda(x_{d_1})h(p'_1(x_{d_1}))(p'_2(x_{d_2}))$. In such a case, there is a correspondence between the syntactic and semantic saturation types of the V and VP expressions. But, the term that renders the sentence at the node (n_0) S, is not algorithmically equivalent to the one in Fig. 3, and naturally reflect on the algorithmic steps that are used during the analyses for filling up arguments. Similarly, the specification terms corresponding to these two options are not algorithmically equivalent.

7 Conclusions and Future Work

We have presented how the formal language of the theory of acyclic recursion L^{λ}_{ar} can be used for semantic representations of natural language via syntax-semantics interface in computational grammar. We have introduced the technique by generalised GCBLG that employs feature-value descriptions. GCBLG is type theoretical by its hierarchy of constraints, which are of dependent types, for the syntactic compositions. The feature-value descriptions embed semantic representations by the higher-order L^{λ}_{ar}-terms. We have focused on two of the major grammar rules for saturation of syntactic and semantic arguments, for underspecified semantic representations of multiple quantifier scopes. A sentence that has two (or more) quantifier NPs, with ambiguous semantic scopes, can be rendered into a single, underspecified L^{λ}_{ar}-term A. The key idea is that A has free recursion variables saturating arguments that can be bound by corresponding quantifier NPs in alternative orders. The phrasal rules of GCBLG introduce restrictions over possible bindings via recursion assignments in syntax-semantics interface.

We foresee extending and implementing the technique for computational syntax-semantics interface in lexical and phrasal structures, for broader grammatical constructions.

References

Bresnan, J. (2001). *Lexical-Functional Syntax.* Oxford: Blackwell Publishers.

Dalrymple, M. (2001). *Lexical Functional Grammar*, Volume 34 of *Syntax and Semantics.* New York: Academic Press.

Joshi, A. K. (1987). An introduction to tree adjoining grammars. *Mathematics of Language 1*, 87–115.

Joshi, A. K., L. S. Levy, and M. Takahashi (1975, February). Tree adjunct grammars. *J. Comput. Syst. Sci. 10*(1), 136–163.

Kroeger, P. (2004). *Analyzing Syntax: A Lexical-Functional Approach.* Cambridge: Cambridge University Press.

Loukanova, R. (2007, August). Typed Lambda Language of Acyclic Recursion and Scope Underspecification. In R. Muskens (Ed.), *Workshop on New Directions in Type-theoretic Grammars*, ESSLLI 2007, Dublin, Ireland, pp. 73–89. The Association for Logic, Language and Information.

Loukanova, R. (2011a). Semantics with the Language of Acyclic Recursion in Constraint-Based Grammar. In G. Bel-Enguix and M. D. Jiménez-López (Eds.), *Bio-Inspired Models for Natural and Formal Languages*, pp. 103–134. Cambridge Scholars Publishing.

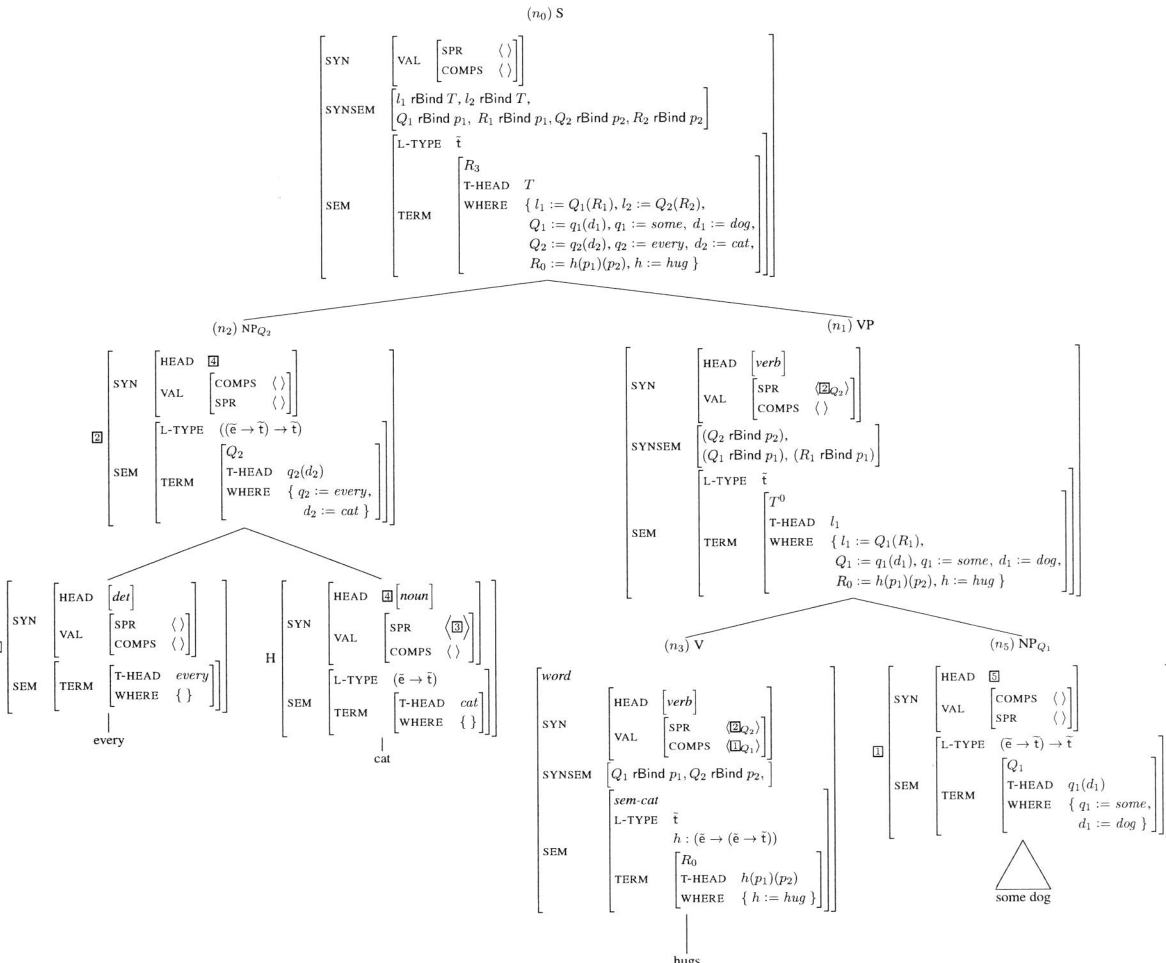

Figure 3: Underspecified Scope: Quantifier NP as Subject and Quantifier NP as Complement

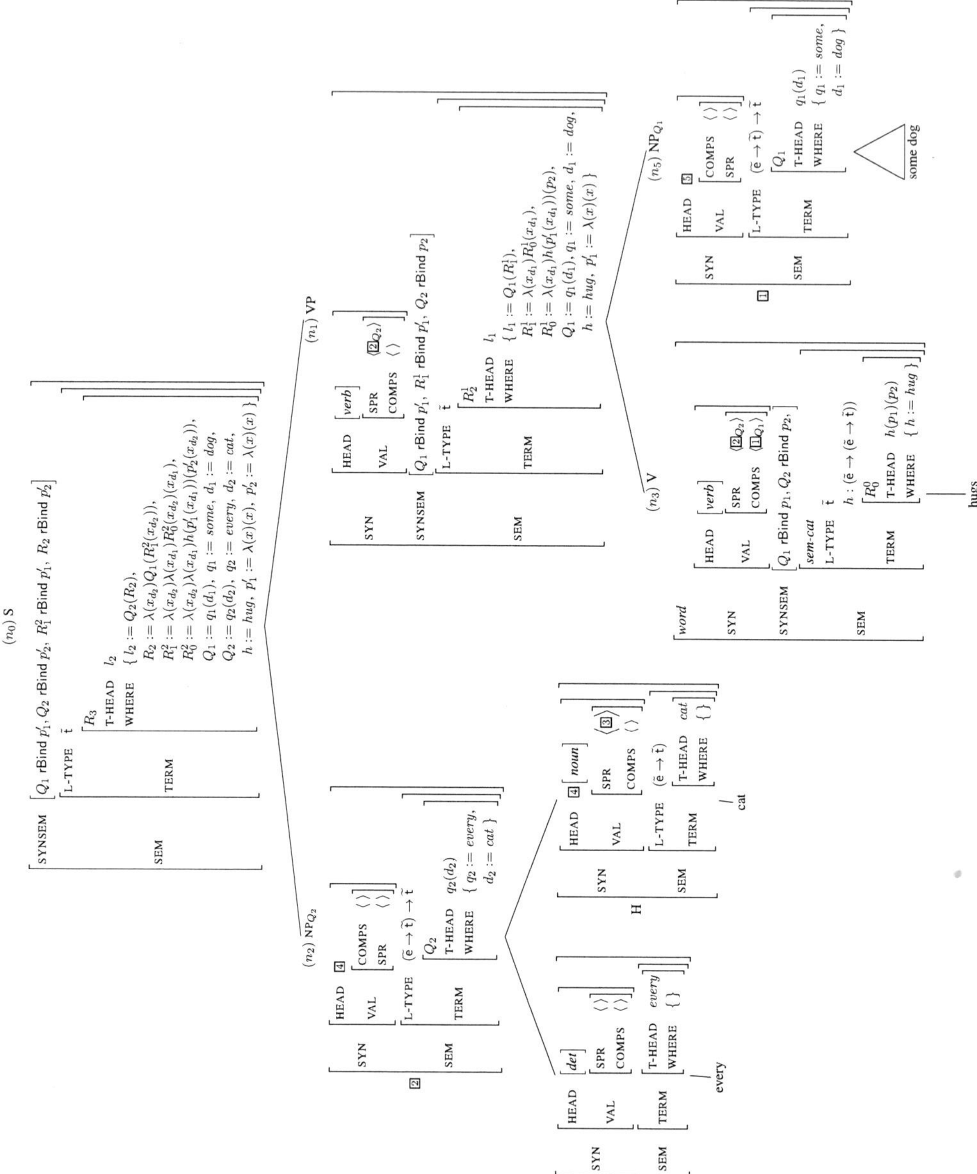

Figure 4: Specification: Quantifier NP as Subject and Quantifier NP as Complement: de dicto

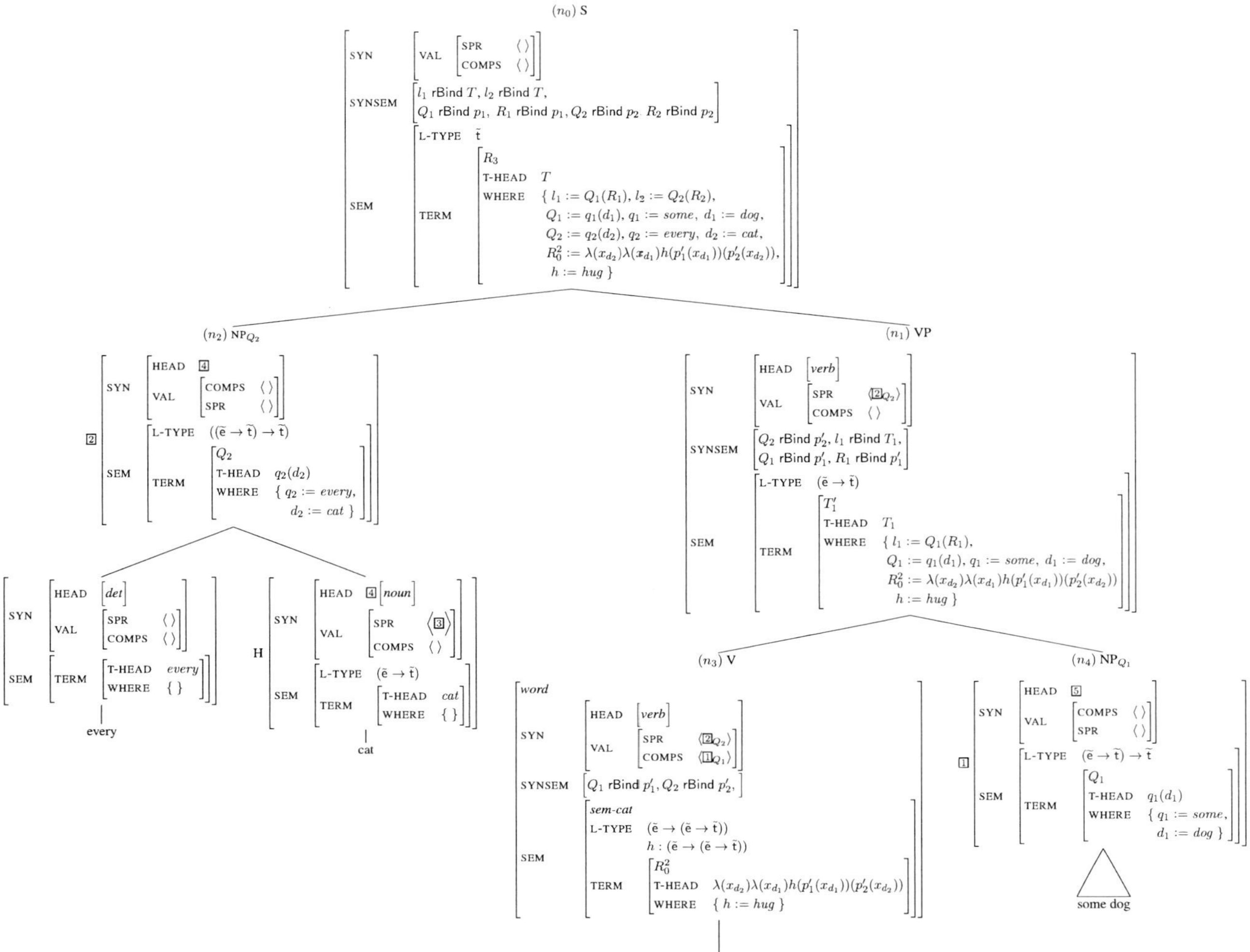

Figure 5: Underspecified Scope: Quantifier NP as Subject and Quantifier NP as Complement: via λ-abstraction

Loukanova, R. (2011b). Syntax-Semantics Interface for Lexical Inflection with the Language of Acyclic Recursion. In G. Bel-Enguix, V. Dahl, and M. D. Jiménez-López (Eds.), *Biology, Computation and Linguistics — New Interdisciplinary Paradigms*, Volume 228 of *Frontiers in Artificial Intelligence and Applications*, pp. 215–236. Amsterdam; Berlin; Tokyo; Washington, DC: IOS Press.

Loukanova, R. (2016). Relationships between Specified and Underspecified Quantification by the Theory of Acyclic Recursion. *ADCAIJ: Advances in Distributed Computing and Artificial Intelligence Journal 5*(4), 19–42.

Loukanova, R. (2017a). An Approach to Functional Formal Models of Constraint-Based Lexicalized Grammar (CBLG). *Fundamenta Informaticae 152*(4), 341–372.

Loukanova, R. (2017b). Binding Operators in Type-Theory of Algorithms for Algorithmic Binding of Functional Neuro-Receptors. In M. Ganzha, L. Maciaszek, and M. Paprzycki (Eds.), *Proceedings of the 2017 Federated Conference on Computer Science and Information Systems*, Volume 11 of *Annals of Computer Science and Information Systems*, pp. 57–66. Polish Information Processing Society.

Loukanova, R. (2018). γ-Reduction in Type Theory of Acyclic Recursion. to appear.

Loukanova, R. (2019). Gamma-star canonical forms in the type-theory of acyclic algorithms. In J. van den Herik and A. P. Rocha (Eds.), *Agents and Artificial Intelligence*, Cham, pp. 383–407. Springer International Publishing.

Moortgat, M. (1996). Categorial type logics. In J. van Benthem and A. ter Meulen (Eds.), *Handbook of Logic and Language*, pp. 93–177. Amsterdam: Elsevier.

Moschovakis, Y. N. (2006). A Logical Calculus of Meaning and Synonymy. *Linguistics and Philosophy 29*(1), 27–89.

Pollard, C. and I. A. Sag (1994). *Head-Driven Phrase Structure Grammar*. Chicago, IL: University of Chicago Press.

Ranta, A. (2011). *Grammatical Framework: Programming with Multilingual Grammars*. Stanford: CSLI Publications.

Sag, I. A., T. Wasow, and E. M. Bender (2003). *Syntactic Theory: A Formal Introduction*. Stanford, California: CSLI Publications.

Vijay-Shanker, K. and D. J. Weir (1994, November). The equivalence of four extensions of context-free grammars. *Mathematical Systems Theory 27*(6), 511–546.

Modeling language constructs with compatibility intervals

Pavlo Kapustin
University of Bergen
pavlo.kapustin@uib.no

Michael Kapustin
Moscow Institute of Physics and Technology
michael.kapustin@gmail.com

Abstract

We describe a representation for modeling meaning of natural language constructs that is closely related to fuzzy sets. Same as fuzzy sets, it allows to express quantitative relationships between different concepts, and is designed to support vagueness and imprecision common to natural language. We compare the representations using several examples, and argue that in some cases the proposed representation may be a good alternative to the fuzzy set based representation, and that it may also be easier to learn from data.

Introduction

Consider the sentence "A young lady came into the room". The word "lady" informs us about the gender of the person, and both words in the construct "young lady" tell us something about the age of the person. To be able to make such inferences one needs quantitative information about the relation of the construct "young lady" to the property "age", i.e. what ages are compatible with this description.

One representation that allows to explicitly capture this type of quantitative information is based on fuzzy sets and suggested by Lotfi Zadeh in his earlier papers (Zadeh, 1971, 1972). However, there is currently not much research in applying this representation to problems of computational linguistics and natural language processing (Carvalho et al., 2012; Novák, 2017).

We believe that one of the reasons for this may be that membership functions are relatively complex objects, possibly increasing the complexity of operations like different transformations and learning from data when using the fuzzy set based representation. In this paper we briefly describe a representation closely related to fuzzy sets that we call compatibility intervals, and argue that in some cases it may be a good alternative to the fuzzy set based representation, and may also be easier to learn from data.

Related work

In his early works, Lotfi Zadeh suggests modeling meaning of certain types of adjectives (e.g. "small", "medium", "large") as fuzzy sets, and some lingustic hedges (e.g. "very", "slightly" — as operators, acting on these fuzzy sets (Zadeh, 1971, 1972). Hersh and Caramazza (1976) introduce logical and linguistic interpretation of membership functions, confirming the difference between them in an experimental setting.

Novák (2017) describes Fuzzy Natural Logic, a mathematical theory attemping to model the semantics of natural language, that includes Theory of Evaluative Linguistic Expressions (Novák, 2008).

In M. Kapustin and P. Kapustin (2015) we describe a framework for computational interpreting of natural language fragments, and suggest modeling meaning of words as operators. P. Kapustin (2015) describes an application that implements and tests some features of this framework in a simplified setting.

Runkler (2016) describes an approach for generation of linguistically meaningful membership functions from word vectors.

In P. Kapustin and M. Kapustin (2019b) we describe a couple of approaches that can be used for modeling meaning of natural language constructs using fuzzy sets and discuss some examples. We

Proceedings of the IWCS 2019 Workshop on Computing Semantics with Types, Frames and Related Structures, pages 49–54
Gothenburg, Sweden, May 24, 2019.

discuss how people relate some language constructs to compatibility intervals in an experimental study (P. Kapustin and M. Kapustin, 2019a).

Schwarzchild and Wilkinson (2002) describe interval-based semantics for comparatives. Abrusán and Spector (2008) describe semantics of degree questions based on intervals.

Different interpretations

Lotfi Zadeh's further work on linguistic variables (Zadeh, 1975a, 1975b, 1975c) and possibility theory (Zadeh, 1999) introduce term "compatibility", clarifying interpretation of the values of the membership functions: they can be seen as degrees of compatibility between the value of the function argument and the construct that is described by the membership function.

Similarly to Hersh and Caramazza (1976), we distinguish between logical and linguistic interpretations of membership functions. Consider fig. 1: "young1" corresponds to the logical interpretation, reflecting the fact that infants and newborns are, indeed, as young as one can be. On the other hand, "young2" corresponds to the linguistic interpretation, reflecting the fact that when we use the word "young", we usually refer to ages other than newborns and infants. Similarly, we normally do not use "often" when something occurs always or almost always, and we normally do not use "seldom" when something occurs never or almost never. On the other hand, the usage of word "old" does not seem to differ from what is "logically" correct: we may say "old" about someone who is 80 or 100 years old.

We think that many, but probably, not all of the differences between logical and linguistic interpretations are related to scalar implicatures and related phenomena, and believe that this needs to be investigated further.

Difference between logical and linguistic interpretations has some interesting implications. Consider fig. 2. Here we apply negation, implemented as Zadeh's complementation (Zadeh, 1972), to constructs "young1", "young2" and "old". While such negation seems to work well with the logical interpretation, it gives somewhat unexpected results with the linguistic interpretation: according to $not(\mu_{\text{young2}})$, it appears that infants are less "not young" than newborns, which is not correct.

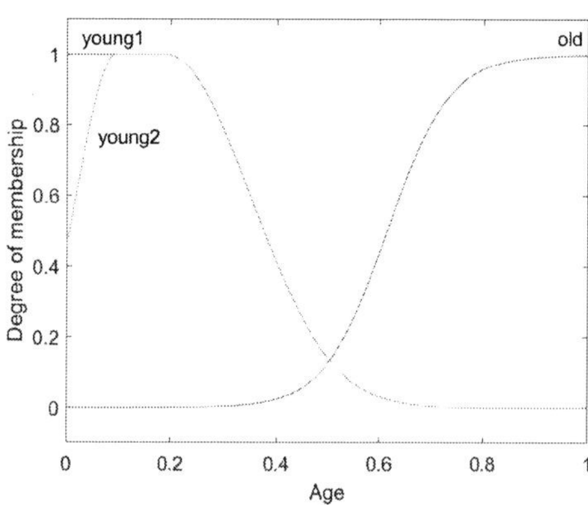

Figure 1: Different meanings of "young".

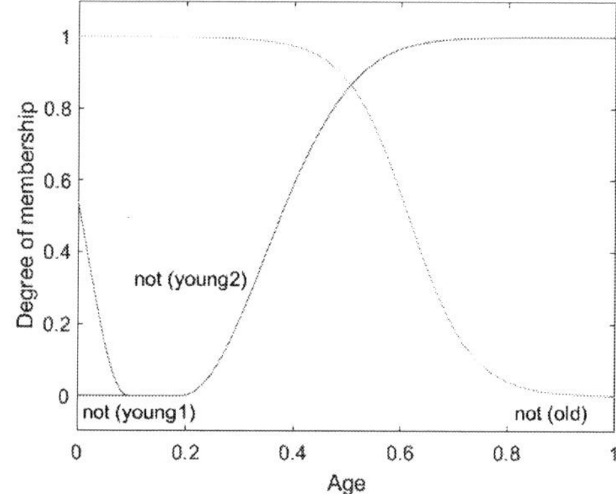

Figure 2: Logical "not", applied to "young1" and "young2".

Consider fig. 3. Here we apply intensifier "very", implemented as Zadeh's concentration (Zadeh, 1972), to constructs "young1", "young2" and "old". While such implementation of "very" seems to work well with the logical interpretation, it gives somewhat unexpected results with the linguistic interpretation: according to $very(\mu_{\text{young2}})$, it appears that infants are "very young" to a lower degree than they are "young". In addition, the width of the interval in which the membership degree is equal to one is unaffected by the application of "very", which seems to be incorrect.

We believe that logical and linguistic interpretations complement each other, each of them modeling different aspects of the meaning of natural language constructs, and for some words may need to be modeled as separate membership functions.

We think that finding mathematical functions and their transformations that correctly capture important details about language constructs may not always be that easy. This seems to become even more challenging if we are working with the linguistic interpretation, as in this case the shape of the functions often becomes more complex.

Representation based on compatibility intervals

Here we briefly describe the representation based on compatibility intervals and discuss some examples.

Compatibility interval is an interval of property values on some scale that are compatible with a given language construct (here term "property" is used in a relatively general sense). The discussion of scales is a large topic of separate research, and is out of scope of this paper.

Compatibility intervals consist of the main subinterval with high compatibility, and optional left ("increasing") and right ("decreasing") subintervals adjacent to the main subinterval. The following invariants are maintained: all the values in the main subinterval have equal (high) compatibility, and the closer the values are to the main subinterval the higher their compatibility is.

Here we provide examples of some intervals for different age groups (we use double hyphens between the start and the end of the main subinterval, and single hyphens between the start and the end of the left and the right subintervals).

```
child: [0 -- 15-20]
young1: [0 -- 30-50]
young2: [0-18 -- 30-50]
adult: [15-20 -- 100]
middle-aged: [40-45 -- 65-70]
old: [70-80 -- 100]
```

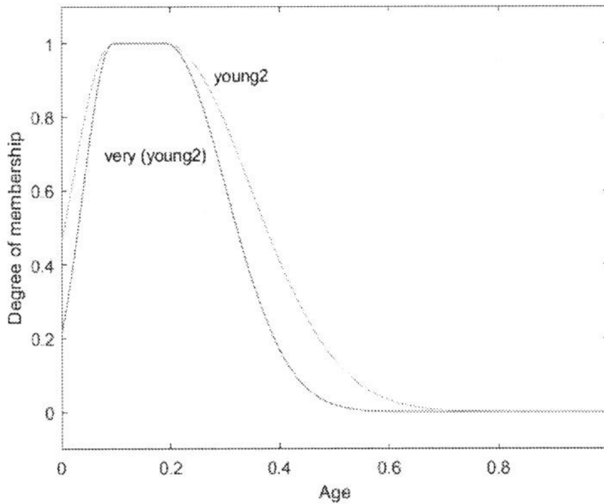

Figure 3: Intensifier "very", applied to "young2".

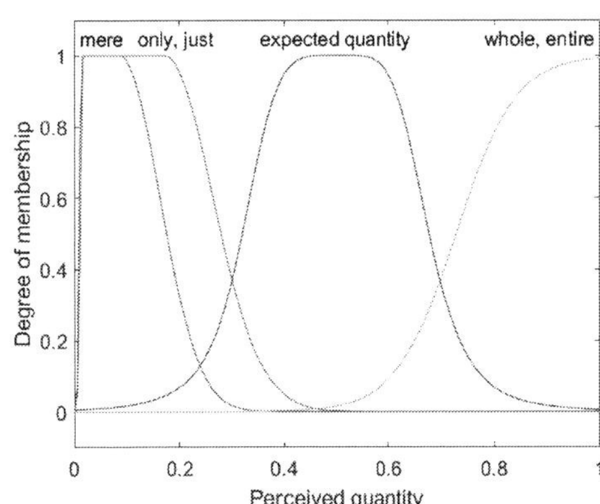

Figure 4: "Mere", "only", "just", "whole" and "entire" related to perceived quantity.

Compatibility intervals may have including or excluding boundaries.

In P. Kapustin and M. Kapustin (2019b) we suggest how words "mere", "only" and "just" can be modeled using fuzzy sets (fig. 4). These words may be used with quantities that are perceived as very small, but not with zero quantities (neither "a mere zero", "only zero" or "only no one" seem to make sense). This fact is not very convenient to model using membership functions. Using the representation based on compatibility intervals, we could model this with an excluding boundary:

```
mere: (0 -- 0.10.3]
```

```
only, just: (0 -- 0.2-0.4]
expected quantity: [0.2-0.4 -- 0.6-0.8]
whole, entire: [0.6-0.8 -- 1]
```

In case of compatibility intervals, instead of using one membership function to model relation of a language construct to a certain property, one or several compatibility intervals can be used (several intervals would correspond to a membership function with more than one maximum, something that could be used for modeling ambiguity). For example, suppose that "teenager" is defined by interval:

```
teenager: [10-13 -- 17-20]
```

Then something corresponding to "not teenager" with meaning similar to Zadeh's complementation (Zadeh, 1972) could be modeled by inverting the interval, for example:

```
[0 -- 10-13)
(17-20 -- 100]
```

Consider the construct "not teenager" in the context of the phrase "you are not a teenager" (that may mean "younger child" or "adult"). Compared to membership functions, as long as intervals don't have membership values, if we would like to represent which of the two intervals corresponding to "not teenager" is more "possible", we would need to store this information separately or extend the representation to optionally contain the membership degree of the main subinterval.

Same as with membership functions, if we are interested in both logical and linguistic interpretations, we need to store two different intervals (or two different sets of intervals, if a construct is represented by several intervals) for some constructs.

Also, as with membership functions, if we attempt to invert interval "young2", trying to model negation similar to Zadeh's complementation (Zadeh, 1972), we would get unexpected results (similar to what is described on fig. 2).

On the other hand, it seems to be easier to model intensifier "very" for the linguistic interpretation using compatibility intervals. If we would like to do something similar to Zadeh's concentration (Zadeh, 1972), we could, for example, use a very simple model: for constructs whose compatibility interval starts at the left end of the scale, we could leave the left boundary of the left subinterval unchanged, multiplying all the other boundaries with a certain factor. For constructs whose compatibility interval ends at the right end of the scale, we could do the opposite: leave the right boundary of the right subinterval unchanged, multiplying all the other boundaries with the inverse of the same factor.

```
young2: [0-18 -- 30-50]
very (young2): [0-16.20 -- 27-45]
old: [60-80 -- 100.0]
very (old): [66.67-88.89 -- 100]
```

Note that we no longer have the unexpected result compared to what was described on fig. 3.

This example is provided to illustrate that it may be easier to control what effects are achieved by doing different transformations when using compatibility intervals, rather than membership functions, because one can move boundaries of the subintervals independently.

Discussion

Presented representation, while being closely related to fuzzy sets, is different in some important respects. Compatibility intervals move attention away from specific mathematical functions, curve shapes and membership degrees, rather focusing on the intervals of values that are compatible with the language construct.

Compared to membership functions, compatibility intervals are relatively simple objects that are defined by several numbers. That's why we hope that certain operations, including different transformations and learning from data, may be easier to implement with compatibility intervals than with fuzzy sets.

We believe that moving focus away from membership degrees has mostly positive effect, as one only needs to think about interval boundaries when implementing operations on intervals. However, we can imagine situations when explicit membership degrees may be desirable. We described one such case related to ambiguity, along with possible solutions.

In general, we think it is positive that there is not a clear boundary between the representation based on fuzzy sets and the representation based on compatibility intervals, which means that it in some cases it may be possible to use benefits of both of the representations.

We discussed why it is important to distinguish between logical and linguistic interpretations when modeling meaning of natural language constructs using fuzzy sets or compatibility intervals.

Representations based on fuzzy sets and compatibility intervals, being closely related, are both able to quantitatively represent what language constructs tell us about certain properties, allowing to capture important aspect of meaning of these constructs. That's why we hope that more researchers in the field of computational linguistics and natural language processing become interested in this area.

Acknowledgements

We thank Vadim Kimmelman and Csaba Veres for helpful discussions and comments. We thank anonymous reviewers for helpful feedback.

References

Abrusán, M., and B. Spector (2008). An interval-based semantics for degree questions: negative islands and their obviation. In *Proceedings of the 27th West Coast Conference on Formal Linguistics, Somerville, MA,* 17–26. Citeseer.

Carvalho, J. P., F. Batista, and L. Coheur (2012). A critical survey on the use of fuzzy sets in speech and natural language processing. In *Fuzzy Systems (FUZZ-IEEE), 2012 IEEE International Conference on,* 1–8. IEEE.

Hersh, H. M., and A. Caramazza (1976). A fuzzy set approach to modifiers and vagueness in natural language. *Journal of Experimental Psychology: General* 105 (3): 254.

Kapustin, M., and P. Kapustin (2015). Modeling meaning: computational interpreting and understanding of natural language fragments. *arXiv preprint arXiv:1505.08149.*

Kapustin, P. (2015). Computational comprehension of spatial directions expressed in natural language. Master's thesis, The University of Bergen.

Kapustin, P., and M. Kapustin (2019a). Language constructs as compatibility intervals: an experimental study. In preparation.

Kapustin, P., and M. Kapustin (2019b). Modeling language constructs with fuzzy sets: some approaches, examples and interpretations. In submission.

Novák, V. (2008). A comprehensive theory of trichotomous evaluative linguistic expressions. *Fuzzy Sets and Systems* 159 (22): 2939–2969.

Novák, V. (2017). Fuzzy logic in natural language processing. In *Fuzzy Systems (FUZZ-IEEE), 2017 IEEE International Conference on,* 1–6. IEEE.

Runkler, T. A. (2016). Generation of linguistic membership functions from word vectors. In *Fuzzy Systems (FUZZ-IEEE), 2016 IEEE International Conference on,* 993–999. IEEE.

Schwarzchild, R., and K. Wilkinson (2002). Quantifiers in comparatives: A semantics of degree based on intervals. *Natural language semantics* 10 (1): 1–41.

Zadeh, L. A. (1971). Quantitative fuzzy semantics. *Information sciences* 3 (2): 159–176.

Zadeh, L. A. (1972). A fuzzy-set-theoretic interpretation of linguistic hedges.

Zadeh, L. A. (1975a). The concept of a linguistic variable and its application to approximate reasoning—I. *Information sciences* 8 (3): 199–249.

Zadeh, L. A. (1975b). The concept of a linguistic variable and its application to approximate reasoning—II. *Information sciences* 8 (4): 301–357.

Zadeh, L. A. (1975c). The concept of a linguistic variable and its application to approximate reasoning-III. *Information sciences* 9 (1): 43–80.

Zadeh, L. A. (1999). Fuzzy sets as a basis for a theory of possibility. *Fuzzy sets and systems* 100 (1): 9–34.

ImageTTR: Grounding Type Theory with Records in Image Classification for Visual Question Answering

Arild Matsson
Språkbanken, Department of Swedish
University of Gothenburg
arild.matsson@gu.se

Simon Dobnik **Staffan Larsson**
CLASP and FLoV
University of Gothenburg
simon.dobnik@gu.se
sl@ling.gu.se

Abstract

We present ImageTTR, an extension to the Python implementation of Type Theory with Records (pyTTR) which connects formal record type representation with image classifiers implemented as deep neural networks. The Type Theory with Records framework serves as a knowledge representation system for natural language the representations of which are grounded in perceptual information of neural networks. We demonstrate the benefits of this symbolic and data-driven hybrid approach on the task of visual question answering.

1 Introduction

A situated artificial conversational agent must be able to interact with its environment through perception and action, as well as with other agents through language. The key challenge for building situated agents is how to represent and reason with both linguistic and non-linguistic information in some formal system that can be modelled on a computer (the question of information fusion). This is challenging because linguistic and perceptual domains are not of the same kind. Perceptional information is typically represented by abundance of sensory readings that are typically represented as real numbers. On the other hand, language is a symbolic system. The two domains are typically bridged through classification (Harnad, 1990).

Several approaches have dealt with information fusion by combining machine learning classification with some kind of formal representation (Kruijff et al., 2006, 2007; Roy, 2005). Recently, using deep learning architectures such associations are learned automatically (Xu et al., 2015; Lu et al., 2016). While they are highly effective, they are not interpretable and directly portable to domains where one would like to combine them with logic-like formal representations.

Among formal representations, first-order logic (FOL) have long been of choice, but it has its limitations. A recent contribution that combines several branches in formal systems is Type Theory with Records (TTR) (Cooper, 2005b, fthc).

The goal of this paper is a model, which is formulated in TTR and connects machine-learning classification of perceptual information on one hand with language on the other, as well as an executable implementation of this model. TTR is expected to represent semantics of perceptual and linguistic content in a single framework. The connection is realised in a visual question answering (VQA) application, where questions are interpreted in the context of an image.

2 Background

2.1 Type Theory with Records (TTR)

Type Theory with Records (TTR) is a formal semantic framework that represents the semantics of language, action and perception (Cooper, fthc). The *types* in type theory are employed to represent words

Proceedings of the IWCS 2019 Workshop on Computing Semantics with Types, Frames and Related Structures, pages 55–64
Gothenburg, Sweden, May 24, 2019.

and semantic units within a sentence or discourse (Cooper, 2005b). A brief introduction to TTR is given in this section. For further reference, see Cooper (2005a) and Cooper (2012).

To begin with, $a : T$ is the judgement that a is of type T. Some *basic types* in TTR are *Ind*, the type of an individual, and Int, the type of integers.

Given that T_1 and T_2 are types, $T_1 \rightarrow T_2$ is a *functional type* whose domain is objects of type T_1 and whose range is objects of type T_2.

Next, we introduce *records* and *record types*. If $a_1 : T_1, a_2 : T_2(a_1), \ldots, a_n : T_n(a_1, a_2, \ldots, a_{n-1})$, where $T(a_1, \ldots, a_n)$ represents a type T which depends on the objects $a_1, \ldots, a_n$, the record to the left in Equation 1 is of the record type to the right. In Equation 1, $\ell_1, \ldots, \ell_n$ are *labels* which can be used elsewhere to refer to the values associated with them. A sample record and record type is shown in Equation 2. If r is a record and ℓ is a label in r, we can use a *path* $r.\ell$ to refer to the value of ℓ in r. Similarly, if T is a record type and ℓ is a label in T, $T.\ell$ refers to the type of ℓ in T. Records (and record types) can be nested, so that the value of a label is itself a record (or record type).

$$r = \begin{bmatrix} \ell_1 & = & a_1 \\ \ell_2 & = & a_2 \\ \ldots & & \\ \ell_n & = & a_n \\ \ldots & & \end{bmatrix} : \begin{bmatrix} \ell_1 & : & T_1 \\ \ell_2 & : & T_2(\ell_1) \\ \ldots & & \\ \ell_n & : & T_n(\ell_1, \ell_2, \ldots, \ell_{n-1}) \end{bmatrix} \tag{1}$$

$$\begin{bmatrix} \text{ref} & = & obj_{123} \\ \text{c}_{\text{man}} & = & \text{prf}(\text{man}(obj_{123})) \\ \text{c}_{\text{run}} & = & \text{prf}(\text{run}(obj_{123})) \end{bmatrix} : \begin{bmatrix} \text{ref} & : & Ind \\ \text{c}_{\text{man}} & : & \text{man(ref)} \\ \text{c}_{\text{run}} & : & \text{run(ref)} \end{bmatrix} \tag{2}$$

As can be seen in Equation 2, types can be constructed from predicates, e.g., "run" or "man". Such types are called *ptypes* and correspond roughly to predicate formulas in first order logic. Ptypes may be *dependent*, which is represented by the fact that arguments to the predicate may be represented by labels used elsewhere. In Equation 2, the type of c_{man} is dependent on ref (as is the type of c_{run}).

A fundamental type-theoretical intuition is that something of a ptype $P(a_1, \ldots, a_n)$ is whatever it is that counts as a proof of $P(a_1, \ldots, a_n)$. One way of putting this is that "propositions are types of proofs". In Equation 2, we simply use prf(P) as a placeholder for proofs of P; below, we will show how perceptual input can be included in proofs[1].

A *singleton type* T_a is a subtype of T restricted so that only a can be a witness of it. In a record type, a singleton-typed field can be written as a *manifest field*: $\begin{bmatrix} \text{x} & : & T_a \end{bmatrix} = \begin{bmatrix} \text{x} = a & : & T \end{bmatrix}$

Types are sorted into orders, where types of one order may be witnesses of a type in a higher order. $\mathit{Type}^n, n > 0$ is the type of all types of order $n - 1$. In this paper, most types will be of order 0, so we will skip the order superscript and use *Type* to denote Type^1. Similar to *Type*, *RecType* is the type of all record types and *PType* is the type of all ptypes.

The *re-labelling* η of a record type T is a set of tuples where the first element is a label in T and the second is another, new label. T_η is the record type which has the same fields as T but where the first item in each element of η has been replaced with the second item. Thus, if $T = \begin{bmatrix} \text{x} & : & T' \end{bmatrix}$ and $\eta = [\langle \text{x}, \text{y} \rangle]$, then $T_\eta = \begin{bmatrix} \text{y} & : & T' \end{bmatrix}$.

A list of objects of type T is a witness of the *list type* list(T): If L is a list and $\forall a \in L, a : T$, then L : list(T). In this paper, the list containing a, b and c will be written as $[a, b, c]$.

2.2 Visual Question Answering (VQA)

Antol et al. (2017) suggest visual question answering (VQA) as a challenge for multi-modal semantic systems. A VQA system is presented an image and a natural-language question about the image, and is expected to produce a natural-language answer. The initiative includes datasets and a series of annual competitions since 2016.

[1]Note that TTR is not proof-theoretic like may other type theories. TTR proofs are more like *witnesses* in situation semantics (Barwise and Perry, 1983) or the *proof objects* in intuitionistic type theory (Martin-Löf and Sambin, 1984).

This task has been defined within the deep learning approach to vision and language. However, a purely end-to-end approach faces challenges like opacity and ignorance of developed models of perception. We choose a hybrid approach to VQA and provide a proof of concept of its strengths in this domain.

Many VQA problems are formulated with open-domain questions. In this paper, however, we are limited to polar (*yes/no*) questions, because those are, arguably, the easiest to model and answer.

It is important to note that the presented model is not an attempt at scoring high in the VQA task. A comparison to dedicated VQA models would place this model low in most aspects: limitations in language domain and syntax, and computation speed, just to name a couple. Rather, this is an exploration of a multimodal representation model (or paradigm), with VQA used as an evaluation context. Advantages of the model include modularity, transparency and reversibility, as provided by the underlying formal-semantic framework.

2.3 Tools

PyTTR (Cooper, 2017) is a Python implementation of TTR. It supports the modelling of TTR types and operations such as judgement and type checking. As a Python library it also enables other features and peripheral procedures to be written in Python. PyTTR allows, in turn, the implementation of TTR models. By implementing a theoretical model as a computer program, it can "come alive" and be tested on real problems and data. When implemented, the model can be evaluated in practical settings.

You Only Look Once (YOLO) (Redmon et al., 2016) is a neural network model for image recognition. Given an image, it will detect objects and classify them. Each detection consists of a bounding box in pixel coordinates, a class label and a confidence score. YOLO is written in C, using the Darknet neural network library (Redmon, 2013). It can be used in Python with the Darkflow library (Trieu, 2018). Development within this thesis has been using the YOLOv2 configuration (Redmon, 2018) trained on the COCO dataset (Lin et al., 2014).

Natural Language Toolkit (NLTK) (Bird et al., 2009) is a Python library facilitating various natural language processing operations. It features a semantically augmented context-free grammar (CFG) framework which enables parsing language into first-order logic (FOL) formulas.

3 A grounded PyTTR

The Python implementation of the model described here is published as a Jupyter notebook file at `https://github.com/arildm/imagettr/releases/tag/1.1` under the open-source MIT license. This section contains references to numbered cells of the notebook file.

3.1 Object detection

The perception of objects in this model is largely based on (Dobnik and Cooper, 2017, Section 5.1). The name and definitions of some of the types have been slightly modified here, for better alignment with the names used in the implementation within this project.

Let the world be of some type $World$, and any portion of the world of some type $Segment$. These types are left undefined for now, as they differ significantly between (Dobnik and Cooper, 2017) and this project. An *object detector* function $f_{objdetector} : ObjDetector$ (Equation 3) maps the world to a collection of *perceptual objects* of the type Obj (Equation 4). A perceptual object contains a segment of the world as well as a field of the type $Ppty$ (Equation 5). A $Ppty$ function can be applied to an individual and return a type, for example $\lambda v : Ind$. kite(v) : $Ppty$. The type $PType$ is defined as the type of all ptypes (Definition 1).

Definition 1 *For any ptype* $T = pred(v_1, ..., v_n)$, $T \sqsubseteq PType$.

$$ObjDetector = (World \to \text{list}(Obj)) \tag{3}$$

$$Obj = \begin{bmatrix} \text{seg} & : & Segment \\ \text{pfun} & : & Ppty \end{bmatrix} \tag{4}$$

$$Ppty = (Ind \to PType) \tag{5}$$

The perceptual object is evidence that a certain segment of the perceptual input is associated with a certain property (such as being a kite). Going further, an *individuation function* $f_{indfun} : IndFun$ (Equation 6) generates an *individuated object* from each perceptual object. The individuated object is a record type and a subtype of $IndObj$ (Equation 7). Here, the 'x' field refers to a specific individual which was only implied by the existence of the perceptual object. The 'cl' field specifies that the position of 'x' is the content of the field 'loc', which has the same type as 'seg' in Obj. Through the 'cp' field, the property can be explicitly associated with the individual.

$$IndFun = (Obj \to RecType) \tag{6}$$

$$IndObj = \begin{bmatrix} \text{x} & : & Ind \\ \text{loc} & : & Segment \\ \text{cp} & : & PType \\ \text{cl} & : & \text{location(x, loc)} \end{bmatrix} \tag{7}$$

Note that the step from the perceptual to the *conceptual* domain is made by generating a record type (not a record), namely the type of *situations* where a certain individual is at a certain location.

3.1.1 Model

This section applies the theory outlined above to the case at hand. The main difference against (Dobnik and Cooper, 2017) is that the world is now an image (Equation 8), rather than a 3D point space. A $Segment$ (Equation 9) is now defined as a record type describing a rectangular bounding box within an image. Its fields contain the centre coordinates of the box ('cx' and 'cy') and the width ('w') and height ('h') of the box.

$$World = Image \tag{8}$$

$$Segment = \begin{bmatrix} \text{cx} & : & Int \\ \text{cy} & : & Int \\ \text{w} & : & Int \\ \text{h} & : & Int \end{bmatrix} \tag{9}$$

The object detection function is a Python function which takes an image as input and invokes YOLO (the implementation of this procedure is in the notebook cells 11, 12 and 14). The return value from YOLO is a collection of dictionary objects, which are converted to perceptual objects of the type Obj which are the output of the object detection function (cell 14, see example in Equation 11).

The individuation function f_{indfun} is defined in Equation 10 (cell 15). Here, the 'x' field is specified as a newly instantiated Ind object a_n, and 'loc' is specified as the perceptual object's 'seg'. The type of the 'cp' field applies the perceptual object's 'pfun' to 'x'. An example output from the function is shown in Equation 12.

$$f_{indfun} = \lambda r : Obj \,.\, \begin{bmatrix} \text{x} = a_n & : & Ind \\ \text{cp} & : & r.\text{pfun(x)} \\ \text{cl} & : & \text{location(x, loc)} \\ \text{loc} = r.\text{seg} & : & Segment \end{bmatrix} \tag{10}$$

$$\begin{bmatrix} \text{seg} & = & \begin{bmatrix} \text{cx} & = & 102 \\ \text{cy} & = & 156 \\ \text{w} & = & 204 \\ \text{h} & = & 84 \end{bmatrix} \\ \text{pfun} & = & \lambda v : Ind \,.\, \text{kite}(v) \end{bmatrix} : Obj \tag{11}$$

$$\begin{bmatrix} \text{x} = a_0 & : & Ind \\ \text{cp} & : & \text{kite(x)} \\ \text{cl} & : & \text{location(x, loc)} \\ \text{loc} = \begin{bmatrix} \text{cx} & = & 102 \\ \text{cy} & = & 156 \\ \text{w} & = & 204 \\ \text{h} & = & 84 \end{bmatrix} & : & Segment \end{bmatrix} \sqsubseteq IndObj \tag{12}$$

3.2 Spatial relations

(Dobnik and Cooper, 2013, Section 3) provides a TTR model of the classification of spatial relations between a located object, a reference object and a viewpoint. The classifier for a given spatial relation may be equal to a geometric classifier κ or this can be combined with functional classifiers to encompass functional aspects of objects on spatial relations (Coventry et al., 2001).

In this project, spatial relation classification is less sophisticated, ignoring the viewpoint as well as the functional aspects of a spatial relation. The reference frame is implicit in the frame of an image, rather than given by a viewpoint object.

A tuple-like record of the type *LocTup* (Equation 13) groups a located object 'lo' and a reference object 'refo'. A classifier of the type *RelClf* (Equation 14) takes a *LocTup* record and returns a new record type which describes the relation.

$$LocTup = \begin{bmatrix} \text{lo} & : & IndObj \\ \text{refo} & : & IndObj \end{bmatrix} \quad (13) \qquad\qquad RelClf = (LocTup \rightarrow RecType) \quad (14)$$

A pattern for a *RelClf* classifier is given in Equation 15, where *rel* is to be replaced with a predicate and κ_{rel} with a boolean classifier.

$$\lambda r : LocTup \, . \begin{cases} \begin{bmatrix} \text{x} & : & r.\text{lo.x} \\ \text{y} & : & r.\text{refo.x} \\ \text{cr} & : & rel(\text{x}, \text{y}) \end{bmatrix}, & \text{if } \kappa_{rel}(r.\text{lo.loc}, r.\text{refo.loc}) \\ [\,], & \text{otherwise} \end{cases} \quad (15)$$

The boolean classifiers are implemented as Python functions, one for each of the relations 'left', 'right', 'above' and 'below'. Each returns true or false after comparing the 'cx' or 'cy' fields of the two *Segment* inputs, i.e. the centre points of the bounding boxes of the objects.

The whole procedure described in this section is implemented in notebook cell 16.

3.3 Beliefs

The set of individuated objects and the set of relation classification results form a set of beliefs. They contain information that the agent has grounded about its perceptual environment. Each of these types is a situation held to be true, by virtue of resulting from perception mechanisms. The belief types are *combined* into one scene record type S which describes the full scene.

3.3.1 Combining situation types

In TTR literature, the combination of multiple record types into one typically follows one of two methods. The first method uses the merge operation $\wedge$ or the asymmetric merge operation $\boxed{\wedge}$. The reliance on field labels in the (asymmetric) merge operation is a problem in this case, where labels have been automatically generated and sometimes clash. Another method is iteratively nesting one record type as a field of the next, and then flattening the result to avoid the nesting. This method avoids label clashes.

However, a third method is used in this project for the purpose of computational speed (cell 18). Each belief record type is re-labelled to only have unique labels, and they are then merged. The resulting type is essentially the same as in the case when nesting and flattening.

3.3.2 De-duplication

Among the belief record types, the same individuals occur more than once. For instance, one belief may hold that a_1 is a kite and another that a_1 is above some other individual. Both beliefs will have a field like $\text{x}_i = a_1 : Ind$, with different labels x_i but the same specification to a_1. *De-duplicating* these is necessary for the subtype check that will follow. This process involves first finding which fields have the same type as another field. Subsequently, simply removing duplicates is not an option, as there may be other fields that depend on the duplicate field. These dependent fields must also first be updated to use the remaining field. This algorithm is implemented in cell 7.

3.4 Parsing user questions

The VQA setting requires the model to understand not only the visual input, but also a natural language question. Parsing natural language is a complex task, ambiguity in syntax as well as semantics being one significant source of difficulties. Within this project, this task has been drastically reduced by focusing on a tiny language domain, with only a handful grammatical constructions and a small, customised vocabulary.

Theoretical formulations of syntactic parsing to TTR have been given in Cooper (2005a,b, 2012, fthc). Applying them in this project is however considered out of scope. Instead, we make use of parsing tools from NLTK (Bird et al., 2009), as follows (cell 20).

A small context-free grammar (CFG) is composed and used to parse natural language into a representation of first-order logic (FOL). The parsing process is visualised in Figure 1. The FOL is then "translated" into a TTR representation by traversing the FOL expression tree and gradually building a TTR record type, according to the following rules: For an *Exists* expression, an *Ind* field is added to the type. For an *Application* expression, a ptype field is added, copying the predicate and variable names. An *And* expression simply triggers recursion into each of the two terms.

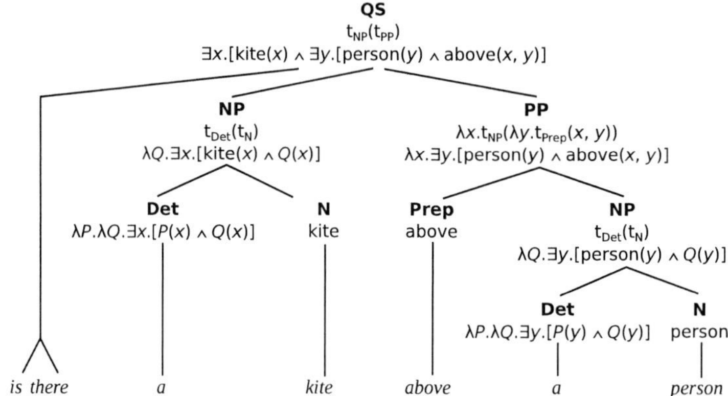

Figure 1: Syntactic-semantic parsing of an utterance into first-order logic. Each node in the tree has a bold-faced constituent label and the FOL lambda expression associated with it. Parent constituents additionally have a third line containing the formula resulting from substitution and β-reduction.

The question sentence in Figure 1 is now translated to the record type Q in Equation 16.

$$Q = \begin{bmatrix} \mathrm{x} & : & \mathit{Ind} \\ \mathrm{y} & : & \mathit{Ind} \\ \mathrm{c}_0 & : & \mathrm{kite(x)} \\ \mathrm{c}_1 & : & \mathrm{person(y)} \\ \mathrm{c}_2 & : & \mathrm{above(x, y)} \end{bmatrix} \tag{16}$$

3.5 Question answering

As a limitation of scope, this project focuses on polar questions. Thus, the language is first limited in domain, to various nouns and geometric spatial relations, and then grammatically, to polar questions.

Object detection and spatial relation classification result in a collection of situation types, which are combined to one, the *scene* type S (Section 3.3). Aside from that, the language parsing results in a type representing the *question* Q (Section 3.4).

The scene type is considered true by virtue of being generated by mechanisms of perceptual classification. The situation described by the question type, on the other hand, will be true if there exists a witness of that type, $r : Q$. It follows that the question type is true if it is a super-type of the scene type, $S \sqsubseteq Q$. Thus, rather than looking for a witness to the question type, we formulate the problem as subtype checking, and answer the question with "yes" or "no" depending on the truth of that check.

An important problem, however, stems from the fact that TTR record types are labelled. In general, fields in the scene type and question type will not share labels in a way that enables direct subtype checking to be useful. Field labels in the scene type will generally not agree with those in the question type. The remedy to this is an alternative subtype relation $\sqsubseteq_{\text{rlb}}$ which is insensitive to label names (cell 21).

Definition 2 *A record type S is a **re-label-subtype** of the record type Q, $S \sqsubseteq_{rlb} Q$, if there is a re-labelling η of Q such that $S \sqsubseteq Q_\eta$.*

An intuitive way to implement this would be to perform all re-labellings η from labels of Q to labels of S and check whether the subtype relation holds. However, this approach is practically impossible, as the number quickly grows very large. An alternative algorithm is developed for the purpose of this project, where fast computation is enabled by making a few assumptions about the input record types[2].

The algorithm handles non-dependent and dependent fields separately. First, when considering re-labellings η of Q, only the non-dependent fields are included. This drastically limits the number of re-labellings to try. Then, for each re-labelling $Q_{\eta'}$ being tried, the remaining, dependent fields are subtype-checked individually, in order to avoid more re-labelling. This means checking person(x) $\sqsubseteq$ person(x) (true) instead of $\left[\text{ c : person(x) }\right] \sqsubseteq \left[\text{ f : person(x) }\right]$ (false). For each dependent field in $Q_{\eta'}$ where there is a field in S that passes this check, the corresponding label pair is added to η'. If, for some $Q_{\eta'}$ field, there is no matching S field, it is concluded that $S \not\sqsubseteq Q_{\eta'}$, and the algorithm proceeds to the next η.

When a re-labelling η is found which enables the subtype check for all dependent fields to pass, the algorithm returns η, which can be interpreted as $S \sqsubseteq_{\text{rlb}} Q$ being true. If all non-dependent-field re-labellings have been evaluated without successful dependent-field subtype checks, the algorithm returns nothing, which is interpreted as the relation not holding.

4 The agent structure

The perceptual-conceptual pieces described above are now connected in an *agent* record type (Equation 17 and Equation 18, cell 21) with associated manipulation algorithms (cell 25). Upon receiving an image, it will carry out object detection, individuation and spatial relation classification, in order to form its beliefs. It may also receive a parsed natural-language utterance, which will then be verified against the beliefs. A construction like this provides a means to answer natural-language questions about the image.

$$Agent = \begin{bmatrix} \text{objdetector} & : & \mathit{ObjDetector} \\ \text{indfun} & : & \mathit{IndFun} \\ \text{relclfs} & : & \text{list}(\mathit{RelClf}) \\ \text{state} & : & \mathit{AgentState} \end{bmatrix} \quad (17) \qquad AgentState = \begin{bmatrix} \text{img} & : & \mathit{Image} \\ \text{perc} & : & \text{list}(\mathit{Obj}) \\ \text{bel} & : & \text{list}(\mathit{RecType}) \\ \text{utt} & : & \mathit{String} \\ \text{que} & : & \mathit{RecType} \end{bmatrix} \quad (18)$$

The fields ‘objdetector’, ‘indfun’ and ‘relclfs’ of *Agent* are to be statically defined for a specific agent. The *AgentState* record in ‘state’ will be modified by the agent algorithm while running. The ‘perc’ field will contain a list of perceptual objects. The ‘bel’ field will be a list of beliefs modelled as situation types: individuated objects and spatial relations between individuals.

For an agent record $ag : Agent$, the perception and question-answering procedure is carried out as follows. Visual input in the form of an image is received, and object detection returns a collection of perceptual objects, for which individuated objects are generated and added as beliefs (Section 3.1). For each pair of individuated objects, spatial relation classifications are generated and also added to beliefs (Section 3.2). Natural-language input is parsed to a type representing the situation hypothesised in the

[2]The algorithm presupposes a certain conformity between S and Q, in that it is not aware of the equivalence between a record type and its flattened version. For instance, it will fail to acknowledge $\left[\, x_1 : \left[\, x_2 : T \,\right] \right] \sqsubseteq_{\text{rlb}} \left[\, x_3 : T \,\right]$. However, this problem is not encountered in this application, due to the the way that S and Q are constructed.

question (Section 3.4). Finally, a re-label-subtype check is performed against the beliefs, and the answer "Yes" or "No" is emitted (Section 3.5).

5 Discussion

Within this project, the foundations of visual question answering (VQA) have been implemented in Type Theory with Records (TTR). The result is an executable application powered by PyTTR.

The application is a practical example that TTR can be used to connect existing vision and language systems. TTR is the single framework that serves as a knowledge representation system that glues together the various parts of the pipeline – perception, language and grounding – and provides reasoning qualified for a simple VQA application.

PyTTR This is one of the few applications of the recently developed PyTTR library. A few extensions were needed in order to realise the present project. Simple and general operations, like copying a record type, could be implemented directly in the PyTTR library. Others, like the combination of record types (Section 3.3.1), should remain in the project-specific source code.

Inference The use of formal frameworks for question-answering tasks, as opposed to statistical or neural methods, especially invites techniques for logical inference. Consider an image of a person wearing glasses, and the question "Does this person have 20/20 vision?" It is reasonable to assume that a person is wearing glasses because they do not have perfect eyesight, to which "20/20 vision" is synonymous. Logical inference, in connection with a database of real-world knowledge encoded in TTR, could help to achieve the synonymity as well as the relationship between eyesight and wearing glasses.

Theorem prover approach to subtype check The re-label-subtype $\sqsubseteq_{\text{rlb}}$ check, currently implemented as an iterative algorithm, could likely be made more efficient and generalised if instead cast as a problem of theorem proving (Plaisted, 2014).

5.1 Future work

Non-polar questions Extending the language domain should be an interesting topic for further research. Keeping within the problem domain of geometric spatial relations, allowing other question types than polar questions is one direction to explore. (Dobnik, 2009, p. 156) lists four basic question types: "Where is the chair?", "Is the table to the left of the chair?" (this is the focus of this project), "What is to the left of the chair?" and "What is the chair to the left of?"

Inference first The algorithm of perception performs classification of spatial relations on all pairs of individuated objects. In other words, all of the agent's beliefs are inferred at once. Later, when attempting to answer the given question, the beliefs can be queried directly in the subtype check. This means spending more effort than sometimes necessary. A more viable alternative is to first parse the question and then perform inference as needed to arrive to an answer. If the question is about the spatial relation between a kite and a person, it will probably be enough to find a kite and a person in the scene, and check that the spatial relation between them matches the one expressed in the question.

Sophisticated spatial relation classification The implementation of spatial relation classification in this project compares the horizontal or vertical coordinates of the centre points of two objects, a simplified geometric representation that does not correspond well to human judgements. A more sophisticated geometric method is the statistical *spatial templates* model (Logan and Sadler, 1996). Another is the *attentional vector-sum (AVS)* model, a mathematical formula which respects object shape (Regier and Carlson, 2001).

References

Antol, S., A. Agrawal, J. Lu, M. Mitchell, D. Batra, C. L. Zitnick, and D. Parikh (2017, May). VQA: Visual Question Answering. *International Journal of Computer Vision 123*(1), 4–31.

Barwise, J. and J. Perry (1983). *Situations and Attitudes*. The MIT Press.

Bird, S., E. Klein, and E. Loper (2009). *Natural Language Processing with Python* (1st ed.). O'Reilly Media, Inc.

Cooper, R. (2005a). Austinian truth, attitudes and type theory. *Research on Language and Computation 3*, 333–362.

Cooper, R. (2005b, April). Records and Record Types in Semantic Theory. *Journal of Logic and Computation 15*(2), 99–112.

Cooper, R. (2012). Type theory and semantics in flux. In R. Kempson, N. Asher, and T. Fernando (Eds.), *Handbook of the Philosophy of Science*, Volume 14: Philosophy of Linguistics. Elsevier BV. General editors: Dov M. Gabbay, Paul Thagard and John Woods.

Cooper, R. (2017). PyTTR. `https://github.com/GU-CLASP/pyttr`.

Cooper, R. (fthc). Type Theory and Language: From Perception to Linguistic Communication. Draft of book chapters available from `https://sites.google.com/site/typetheorywithrecords/drafts` (accessed on 2018-01-17), University of Gothenburg.

Coventry, K., M. Prat-Sala, and L. Richards (2001, April). The Interplay between Geometry and Function in the Comprehension of Over, Under, Above, and Below. *Journal of Memory and Language 44*, 376–398.

Dobnik, S. (2009). *Teaching Mobile Robots to Use Spatial Words*. Ph. D. thesis, The Queen's College, University of Oxford.

Dobnik, S. and R. Cooper (2013, March). Spatial Descriptions in Type Theory with Records. In *Proceedings of IWCS 2013 Workshop on Computational Models of Spatial Language Interpretation and Generation (CoSLI-3)*, Potsdam, Germany, pp. 1–6. Association for Computational Linguistics.

Dobnik, S. and R. Cooper (2017). Interfacing Language, Spatial Perception and Cognition in Type Theory with Records. *Journal of Language Modelling 5*(2), 273–301.

Harnad, S. (1990, June). The symbol grounding problem. *Physica D 42*(1–3), 335–346.

Kruijff, G.-J. M., J. D. Kelleher, and N. Hawes (2006). Information fusion for visual reference resolution in dynamic situated dialogue. In E. André, L. Dybkjær, W. Minker, H. Neumann, and M. Weber (Eds.), *Perception and Interactive Technologies. International Tutorial and Research Workshop, PIT 2006 Kloster Irsee, Germany*, pp. 117–128. Berlin, Heidelberg: Springer.

Kruijff, G.-J. M., H. Zender, P. Jensfelt, and H. I. Christensen (2007). Situated dialogue and spatial organization: what, where... and why? *International Journal of Advanced Robotic Systems 4*(1), 125–138.

Lin, T.-Y., M. Maire, S. Belongie, J. Hays, P. Perona, D. Ramanan, P. Dollár, and C. L. Zitnick (2014). Microsoft COCO: Common Objects in Context. In D. Fleet, T. Pajdla, B. Schiele, and T. Tuytelaars (Eds.), *Computer Vision – ECCV 2014*, Volume 8693, pp. 740–755. Cham: Springer International Publishing.

Logan, G. D. and D. D. Sadler (1996). A computational analysis of the apprehension of spatial relations. In *Language and Space.*, Language, speech, and communication., pp. 493–529. Cambridge, MA, US: The MIT Press.

Lu, J., C. Xiong, D. Parikh, and R. Socher (2016). Knowing when to look: Adaptive attention via a visual sentinel for image captioning. *arXiv arXiv:1612.01887 [cs.CV]*, 1–10.

Martin-Löf, P. and G. Sambin (1984). *Intuitionistic type theory.* Studies in proof theory. Bibliopolis.

Plaisted, D. A. (2014, March). Automated theorem proving: Automated theorem proving. *Wiley Interdisciplinary Reviews: Cognitive Science 5*(2), 115–128.

Redmon, J. (2013). Darknet: Open Source Neural Networks in C. `https://pjreddie.com/darknet/` (accessed on 2018-09-21).

Redmon, J. (2018, September). YOLO: Real-Time Object Detection. `https://pjreddie.com/darknet/yolov2/` (accessed on 2018-09-21).

Redmon, J., S. Divvala, R. Girshick, and A. Farhadi (2016, June). You Only Look Once: Unified, Real-Time Object Detection. In *2016 IEEE Conference on Computer Vision and Pattern Recognition (CVPR)*, Las Vegas, NV, USA, pp. 779–788. IEEE.

Regier, T. and L. A. Carlson (2001, June). Grounding Spatial Language in Perception: An Empirical and Computational Investigation. *Journal of Experimental Psychology: General 130*(2), 273–298.

Roy, D. (2005, September). Semiotic schemas: a framework for grounding language in action and perception. *Artificial Intelligence 167*(1-2), 170–205.

Trieu, T. H. (2018, March). Darkflow. `https://github.com/thtrieu/darkflow` (accessed on 2018-09-21).

Xu, K., J. Ba, R. Kiros, A. Courville, R. Salakhutdinov, R. Zemel, and Y. Bengio (2015, February 11). Show, attend and tell: Neural image caption generation with visual attention. *arXiv arXiv:1502.03044 [cs.LG]*, 1–22.

Enthymemetic Conditionals: Topoi as a guide for acceptability

Eimear Maguire
Laboratoire Linguistique Formelle (UMR 7110), Université de Paris
eimear.maguire@etu.univ-paris-diderot.fr

Abstract

To model conditionals in a way that reflects their acceptability, we must include some means of making judgements about whether antecedent and consequent are meaningfully related or not. Enthymemes are non-logical arguments which do not hold up by themselves, but are acceptable through their relation to a topos, an already-known general principle or pattern for reasoning. This paper uses enthymemes and topoi as a way to model the world-knowledge behind these judgements. In doing so, it provides a reformalisation (in TTR) of enthymemes and topoi as networks rather than functions, and information state update rules for conditionals.

1 Introduction

The content of the antecedent and consequent of a conditional, not just their truth or falsity, makes a difference to whether we find the conditional acceptable or not, generally rejecting those that seem disconnected (Douven, 2008). If we are to model conditionals in a way that reflects their acceptability, we must include some means of making those judgements. Enthymemes are non-logical arguments which are nevertheless treated as acceptable through their relation to a topos, a general principle or pattern for reasoning. Apart from the evidence from their own acceptability conditions, which correlate strongly with judgements of high conditional probability, conditional structures are also associated with 'that kind of thinking', being used as plain-language explanations of particular topoi (e.g. "if something is a bird, then it flies" in Breitholtz, 2014b), or used as materials on reasoning in any number of experiments (e.g. Pijnacker et al., 2009). If we are going to explicitly recognise the use of such 'rule' type objects in discourse, then conditionals are one place where they show up, at least sometimes.

This paper has two aims. First, to propose a formalisation of enthymemes and topoi that is geared towards relating them to more complex rule-based world knowledge, including a distinction between knowledge about causality, non-causality, and ambiguity about causality. Second, to account for the acceptability (or not) of conditionals by proposing an enthymeme-like structure as associated with *if*-conditionals, such that topoi can enhance their content and are used in judging whether a given conditional is acceptable or not. The acceptability of conditionals is linked to perceived relationships between the antecedent and consequent cases: with enthymemes and topoi, we can incorporate this non-arbitrarily into the dialogue state.

The rest of this section will provide some background. Section 2 is focused on enthymemes, topoi, and specification of the alternative formalism, while Section 3 uses this in a proposal of update rules associated with conditionals. Lastly, Section 4 provides a conclusion. This paper draws on work on enthymemes and topoi elsewhere in Breitholtz (2014a,b) etc, and will likewise use TTR (Cooper, 2012) for formalisation.

1.1 Enthymemes and Topoi

Enthymemes are incomplete non-logical arguments that get treated as complete ones. They are 'incomplete' in that to be accepted, they must be identified as a specific instance of a more general pattern that is already in the agent's resources – a topos. Topoi encode world knowledge that comes as a 'rule of

Proceedings of the IWCS 2019 Workshop on Computing Semantics with Types, Frames and Related Structures, pages 65–74
Gothenburg, Sweden, May 24, 2019.

thumb', such as characteristics typical of groups, and a speaker may hold contradictory topoi as equally valid in different scenarios, with no clash experienced unless both are used at the same time. Speakers make enthymemetic arguments by linking what on the surface might technically be non-sequiturs, but are easily identified as an argument using accepted principles. For example, a speaker might say "Let's go left here, it's a shortcut". This argument invokes the assumption that shorter routes are better, and that therefore the left turn being a shortcut is a good reason to take it – but they might equally say "it's longer", invoking an assumption that a longer route is preferable.

Topoi have been proposed to be a resource available to speakers, and consequently a means to address non-monotonic reasoning (Breitholtz, 2014b), the treatment of non-logical rules as expressing necessity, and contradictory claims being equally assertable, as in the route-taking example above Breitholtz (2014a).

To these ends, they have been formalised in TTR for use in dialogue (Breitholtz and Cooper, 2011), as functions from records to record types, as in this example (Breitholtz, 2014a):

(1) a. *Topos:*

$$\lambda r : \begin{bmatrix} x & : \mathit{Ind} \\ c_{bird} & : \text{bird}(x) \end{bmatrix} \left(\begin{bmatrix} c_{fly} & : \text{fly}(r.x) \end{bmatrix} \right)$$

b. *Enthymeme:*

$$\lambda r : \begin{bmatrix} x = \text{Tweety} & : \mathit{Ind} \\ c_{bird} & : \text{bird(x)} \end{bmatrix} \left(\begin{bmatrix} c_{fly} & : \text{fly(Tweety)} \end{bmatrix} \right)$$

Both are of type *Rec* → *RecType*, and the fields of the specified record types match, but fields of the enthymeme have been restricted to specific values. A function to a record type does not by itself indicate what happens once we have access to that type, such as gaining a belief that some instance of it exists (e.g. that there really some case where the bird flies). For these functions to be useful, they are additionally governed by a theory of action, which will license various actions that can be performed with the type, e.g. judging that the original situation is additionally of that type, judging that there exists some situation of the type described, or creating something of that type (Cooper, in prep).

1.2 Conditionals

The assumption that conditionals express a proposition is fundamental to most linguistic work on the topic, both that which follows the commonly accepted restrictor theory of conditional semantics based on the work of Lewis (1975), Kratzer (1986) and Heim (1982), and that which does not (e.g. Gillies, 2010).

As mentioned at the beginning, the acceptability of conditionals correlates strongly with their conditional probability, with Stalnaker (1970) proposing that the probability of a conditional and the conditional probability of the consequent on the antecedent are one and the same, in what is usually referred to as *the Equation*. A subsequent proof by Lewis (1976) found that there is no single proposition based on the antecedent and consequent such that its probability will consistently match the conditional probability. Therefore one could have a propositional theory of conditionals, or validate the Equation – but not both.

However, conditional probability seems so important to the meaning of conditionals that in the view of some non-linguists, (e.g. Edgington, 1995; Bennett, 2003) conditionals should properly be considered be probabilistic, directly expressing the conditional probability of the consequent on the antecedent, P(*cons*|*ant*). Subsequent empirical work overwhelmingly supports the intuition behind the original Equation, and shows that conditional probability does indeed tend to correlate with acceptability (e.g. Evans et al., 2003; Oaksford and Chater, 2003). Conditional probability thus needs to be taken seriously, whether one believes it is the core content of a conditional or not: indeed, figuring out how propositional theories can accommodate its relationship to acceptability is an important issue (e.g. Douven and Verbrugge, 2013). Conditional probability is also not the only factor in acceptability: it is further moderated by whether there appears to be a connection between antecedent and consequent (Skovgaard-Olsen et al., 2016). To make these judgements, we need to know about the relationships between the antecedent and consequent states.

2 Enthymemes, Topoi and Other Knowledge

Given that their presence in an agent's resources has already been motivated, topoi are a natural way to account for the required knowledge about some 'dependence' between antecedent and consequent. Enthymemes and topoi are snippets of reasoning, rather than complex networks, but they should also be related explicitly to other rule-like world knowledge, which includes the possibility of multiple relationships between more than two cases, and knowledge of explicitly causal relations. If we are going to use topoi to express the kind of knowledge that also forms such networks (i.e. informative about causality or related probabilities in more complex systems), then they should be in the same form as that knowledge. The alternative, to keep succinct rule-like topoi apart from larger rule-based(ish) systems, is counter-intuitive.

Bayesian networks (a combination of directed acyclic graphs and probability distributions) are a common way to encode causal relations. They have two components, the first of which is a directed acyclic graph, with the various variables as nodes, and directed edges describing any direct relationships. Graphs and networks are a useful way to describe relationships, and express a more complex set of relationships than a linear chain of functions. The graph structure is in accordance with constraints about what direct parenthood in the graph can mean – that the parent is part of the minimal set of preceding nodes whose value determines the probability distribution of the child.

The second component to a Bayesian Network is a set of probability functions for determining the values of variables given the values of their parents – their conditional probabilities. Associated probabilities are also a natural means of modelling learning, by adjusting the confidence in a given rule on the basis of evidence and experience, allow us to make explicit the level of confidence in a judgement beyond a binary. For unreliable rules, a high (but below 1) probability can be used to express that they are likely to be correct in a given case, but not certain.

2.1 Graphical Topoi

The proposal is as follows. Topoi and enthymemes are of the same type as any other 'relational' knowledge, by which I mean knowledge about causal and correlational relations. This knowledge can be encoded as a graph. The direction(s) of the links between connected nodes, along with additional constraints, indicate either causal or non-causal relations via directed or bi-directed links respectively. The variable at each node is a $RecType$, representing a situation, with the probability of a $RecType$ being across whether it is true or false (for type *T*, whether $\exists a : T$). Topoi and enthymemes as usually discussed are minimal examples, containing only two nodes.

Let $RecType_i$ be a *RecType* associated with an index, and *ProbInfo* be a constraint on some probability. The supertype of enthymemes and topoi, rather than a function *Rec→RecType*, is the type *Network*:

$$\text{(2)}\quad \textit{Network} =_{def} \begin{bmatrix} \text{nodes} : \left\{\textit{RecType}_i\right\} \\ \text{links} : \left\{\langle \textit{RecType}_i, \textit{RecType}_i\rangle\right\} \\ \text{probs} : \left\{\text{ProbInfo}\right\} \\ \text{c}_{index} : \exists\langle x'_j, y_p\rangle, \langle x''_k, z_q\rangle \in \text{links}, x'_j, x''_k \sqsubseteq_r x_i \in \text{nodes}, \\ \quad i = j = k. \text{ Likewise for } \langle y_p, x'_j\rangle, \langle z_q, x''_k\rangle \in \text{links} \\ \quad \text{and } \langle x'_j, y_p\rangle, \langle z_q, x''_k\rangle \in \textit{links}. \\ \text{c}_{links} : \forall\langle x'_i, y'_p\rangle \in \text{links}, \exists x_i, y_p \in \text{nodes}, x'_i \sqsubseteq_r x_i, y'_p \sqsubseteq_r y_p \end{bmatrix}$$

Let $\sqsubseteq_r$ indicate a subtype relation where subtyping is through restriction of one or more fields i.e. not through the specification of extra fields. The first constraint c_{index} enforces co-indexing, that if subtypes of a node are included in *links*, they all share its index. The second constraint c_{links} specifies that any members of *links* are between (potentially restricted subtypes of) members of $nodes$. For ease of reading and the sake of space, the constraints will not be repeated in further examples. In a link $\langle x_i, x_j\rangle$, the specification of member x_i may use j to indicate some $r : x_j$, and vice versa, e.g. where a is some field in x_i and b is some field in x_j, specifying that $a = j.b$.

Causality, non-causal correlation and independence are interpreted on the basis of the members of *links*. Where a path is a sequence of indices $\langle 1, \ldots, k\rangle$ such that for each $i, i+1$ there is $\langle x_i, x_{i+1}\rangle \in$ *links*, the node indexed i is a predecessor of the node indexed j (shorthand: *predecessor*$(i, j,$ *links*)) if there is a path from i to j, given the contents of *links*. Where there is a bi-directional link e.g. $\langle x_i, x_j\rangle, \langle x_j, x_i\rangle \in$ *links*, the relationship is non-causal. Where there is an absence of any path, the relationship may be treated as potential independence. Where there is a link in one direction only, the relationship may be treated as potentially causal. However, neither this potential independence or causality is locked in: there is a distinction between merely lacking information, and having information about a confirmed absence. Certainty about independence or causality is expressed via constraints preventing the addition of any link that would violate them. For n : *Network* containing nodes x_i and x_j, independence, causality and non-causality can be expressed in updated n' as follows, where $a \wedge b$ indicates the merge of two records, a record containing all fields from both, and $a\boxed{\wedge}b$ indicates their asymmetric merge (see Cooper and Ginzburg (2015)), where in event of a field appearing in both records, the field from b is the one found in the merge, effectively overwriting the field of a.

(3) *Independence of i and j:*

$$n' = n\wedge\left[\mathrm{c}_{ind_{ij}} : \neg predecessor(i, j, links) \wedge \neg predecessor(j, i, links)\right]$$

(4) *Direct causality from i to j:*

$$n' = n\wedge\left[\mathrm{c}_{cause_{ij}} : \langle i, j\rangle \in n.links \wedge \neg predecessor(j, i, links)\right]$$

(5) *Non-causality between i and j, where* $\langle x_i, x_j\rangle \in$ *n.links:*

$$n' = n\boxed{\wedge}\left[\text{links} = \text{n.links} \cup \langle x_j, x_i\rangle : \left\{\langle RecType_i, RecType_i\rangle\right\}\right]$$

The choice of bi-directed rather than undirected edges to express non-causality is motivated by a desire for the difference in belief from potentially causal to non-causal to be something that changes easily (i.e. with the addition of information, not replacement of one thing with another of a different type), and for creation of a 'casual' (not a typo) middle-ground, where only one direction is of relevance and there is no strong commitment either way.

All this is meant to allow for a more complex set of relationships than expressed in your average topos which, as stated earlier, is a minimal case with just two nodes. The original example can now be rewritten as follows:

(6) *Topos:*

$$\begin{bmatrix} \text{nodes} = \left\{ \begin{bmatrix} \text{x : Ind} \\ \mathrm{c}_{bird} : \text{bird(x)} \end{bmatrix}^{1}, \begin{bmatrix} \text{x : Ind} \\ \mathrm{c}_{fly} : \text{fly(x)} \end{bmatrix}^{2} \right\} : \left\{RecType_i\right\} \\ \text{links} = \left\{ \left\langle \begin{bmatrix} \text{x : Ind} \\ \mathrm{c}_{bird} : \text{bird(x)} \end{bmatrix}^{1}, \begin{bmatrix} \textbf{x = 1.x} : \text{Ind} \\ \mathrm{c}_{fly} : \text{fly(x)} \end{bmatrix}^{2} \right\rangle \right\} : \left\{\langle RecType_i, RecType_i\rangle\right\} \\ \text{probs} = \left\{ \text{P}\left(\begin{bmatrix} \textbf{x = r.x} : \text{Ind} \\ \mathrm{c}_{fly} : \text{fly(x)} \end{bmatrix}^{2} \mid \text{r} : \begin{bmatrix} \text{x : Ind} \\ \mathrm{c}_{bird} : \text{bird(x)} \end{bmatrix}^{1} \right) = 0.95 \right\} : \left\{\text{ProbInfo}\right\} \end{bmatrix}$$

(7) *Enthymeme:* as the topos, but all variants indexed with i are replaced with

$$\begin{bmatrix} \textbf{x = Tweety} : \text{Ind} \\ \mathrm{c}_{bird} : \text{bird(x)} \end{bmatrix}^{1}$$

The confidence rating of 0.95 has been somewhat arbitrarily set here for topoi to imply high confidence without certainty. Enthymemes are distinguished from other arguments by the fact they don't hold up by themselves, but are instead accepted on the basis of identification with a topos – this doesn't include arguments that are accepted despite being unsupported. However, the terms enthymeme and topoi will continue to be used here: this is partly for convenience, but also because once the context indicates that an enthymemetic argument is being made (such as a recognisable suggestion+motivation pattern), an unsupported 'enthymeme', once accepted, can be used to establish a potential new topos (Breitholtz, 2015). An *Enth* is defined as a *Network* containing a node that has at least one field restricted to a specific object, removing its generality. A *Topos* is a *Network* in which no fields are restricted to a specific object.

An enthymeme e may be identified with a topos t if its nodes and links have equivalents in t, that is if for every node $x_i \in e.nodes, \exists y_p \in t.nodes$ such that $x_i \sqsubseteq y_p$ and for any links $\langle x'_i, x'_j\rangle \in e.links, \exists\langle y'_p, y'_q\rangle \in t.links$ such that $x'_i \sqsubseteq y'_p$ and $x'_j \sqsubseteq y'_q$. This may be by a clear match for the topos fields, but may also include the types of fields in the enthymeme as subtypes of fields in the topos[1].

[1] as in the example "Give a coin to the porter, he carried the bags all the way here" from Breitholtz (2014b), where carrying

3 Conditionals and Reasoning

Having reformalised topoi and enthymemes as an object intended for more general correlational and causal knowledge, we turn back to conditionals.

Firstly, and as mentioned at the beginning, expressing this kind of relational knowledge is (both intuitively and according to empirical evidence) strongly associated with conditionals, and existence of a dependence relation and high conditional probability usually determine their acceptability. Van Rooij and Schulz (2019) suggest a way to combine these two features into a single measure, the relative difference the state of the parent in a relation makes to the likelihood of the child. Pleasingly, with some independence assumptions this measure works not only for the 'causal' direction typically expressed by conditionals (*if there's fire, there's smoke*), but for the reverse as expressed by evidential conditionals (*if there's smoke, there's fire*). However, for it to do so, the direction of the relationship still has to be recognised even when the 'usual' roles of antecedent as parent and consequent as child have flipped. This kind of structural knowledge is topoic.

Secondly, and while it feels almost trivial to point out, we use conditionals to tell each other new things. When we are informed of something through the use of a conditional, we don't necessarily know beforehand that they lie in such a relation: otherwise they would only be useful to draw attention to connections we haven't made, not to tell each other things that are entirely new. Indeed, Skovgaard-Olsen et al. (2016) found evidence that when faced with a conditional, people assume that there is a positive connection between antecedent and consequent unless they have reason to believe otherwise. It is not so much that an acceptable conditional has to be backed up by pre-existing knowledge about the relation between the antecedent and consequent cases, but at the very least it should not *clash* with any.

Breitholtz (2014a) mentions how an enthymemetic argument can be recognised on the basis of the current conversational game/expected rules (with the specific example of knowledge that a suggestion may be followed by the speaker providing a motivation), or by an explicit lexical cue. With the above in mind, I will suggest that use of an *if*-conditional is one such linguistic cue.

3.1 Enthymemetic Conditionals

The overall suggestion is as follows. *If*-conditionals are associated with the making of enthymeme-like arguments. Note that I say "enthymeme-*like* arguments", not "enthymemetic arguments". Enthymemes depend on identification with a previously-known topos, while conditionals can be used to teach new relations, rather than just make statements that rely on existing knowledge to make sense. Although they are structured like the characterisation of enthymemes and topoi above, they are not all strictly speaking 'enthymemetic'. The content of a conditional can be checked against the topoi in the agent's resources. Given a match with a topos, an enhanced version can be added to the agent's knowledge if a link is found between the two relevant nodes. If no supporting topos is found, a more minimal version can be added without the benefit of any extra details a topos might have provided. If there only exists a match for the nodes in a topos that specifies there is definitely no link between them, or that there is a conflicting link, then the conditional should be rejected. The following subsections describe dialogue state update rules associated with conditionals.

3.2 Use of a conditional

To begin with, the type of an information state is minimally given as (8), broadly following the decisions for the place of enthymemes and topoi in Breitholtz (2014a) etc.

(8) *InfoState* $=_{def}$

$$\begin{bmatrix} \text{priv} & : \begin{bmatrix} \text{Topoi} & : \{\text{Topos}\} \end{bmatrix} \\ \text{dgb} & : \begin{bmatrix} \text{enths} & : \{\text{Enth}\} \\ \text{Topoi} & : \{\text{Topos}\} \\ \text{Moves} & : \text{list(LocProp)} \end{bmatrix} \end{bmatrix}$$

someone else's bags is recognised as a subtype of work, and the enthymemetic argument is on the basis of a topos like *work should be rewarded*

(9) *Prop* $=_{def}$

$$\begin{bmatrix} \text{sit} & : \textit{Rec} \\ \text{sit-type} & : \textit{RecType} \end{bmatrix}$$

(10) *Update rule* $=_{def}$

$$\begin{bmatrix} \text{pre} & : \text{InfoState} \\ \text{effects} & : \text{Infostate} \end{bmatrix}$$

The information state has two parts: the agent's private resources, and their representation of the shared context. The *private* resources include propositions[2] and specific relations about which they have beliefs, and a set of general topoi which they can use as resources. Fields for beliefs about propositions and for private beliefs about specific enthymemes have been omitted from the above as we will not need to reference them, although propositions themselves will appear in example (14) later. A public *Topoi* field tracks which topoi have been introduced onto the dialogue gameboard. The general form for update rules is given in (10): *pre* describes the preconditions for states to which the rule can be applied, and *effects* the changes.

Next we will add a few useful functions on the basis of some of the content of Section 2.1: a means to describe whether there is a successful match between an enthymeme and a topos, and a means to reference the result of an enthymeme that has been enriched by the content of a topos.

(11) *enthMatch*(e : Enth, t : Topos) : Bool, **true** iff all of the following hold

(i) All e's nodes are subtypes of t's nodes:
$\forall x_i \in e.nodes, \exists y_p \in t.nodes$ such that $x_i \sqsubseteq y_p$,

(ii) All e's links are subtypes of t's links:
$\forall \langle x'_i, x'_j \rangle \in e.links, \exists \langle y'_p, y'_q \rangle \in t.links$ such that $x'_i \sqsubseteq y'_p$ and $x'_j \sqsubseteq y'_q$,

(iii) For any constraints on links in e, the same constraints hold for the equivalent links in t:
$\forall c_{ind_{ij}} \in e, \exists c_{ind_{pq}} \in t$ or $c_{ind_{qp}} \in t$,
$x_i \in e.nodes, y_p \in t.nodes, x_i \sqsubseteq y_p$ and $x_j \in e.nodes, y_q \in t.nodes, x_j \sqsubseteq y_q$.
Likewise for all $c_{cause_{ij}} \in e$, there is an equivalent $c_{cause_{pq}} \in t$.

(12) *enhanceEnth*(e : Enth, t : Topos) : Enth, e' such that e' is an asymmetric merge of t and e, where the sets in *nodes*, *links* and *probs* undergo asymmetric union such that for any nodes $x_i \in e.nodes, y_p \in t.nodes, x_i \sqsubseteq y_p$, the corresponding node $z_u \in e'.nodes = y_p \boxed{\wedge} x_i$.
Likewise for any subtypes x'_i and y'_p, $x'_i \sqsubseteq y'_p$ in members of $e.links$, $t.links$, $e.probs$ and $t.probs$.

The update rules for each case are given in the subsections below. These are rules for 'specific' conditionals, not those expressing general rules such as *if there's fire, there's smoke*. There should be an equivalent to each rule below for a conditional that expresses a general topos, on the basis of whether any fields in the conditional's content are tied to a specific object. These should lead to an update of *Topoi* only, not of *enths*. They are not included here, and the rules below don't include explicit constraints for steering the update into *enths* only where a check for a restricted field is successful. There are three rules given: where there is a supporting topos in the 'default' direction, where there is not but there is a supporting topos in the reverse direction, and where there is neither support nor a clash.

3.2.1 Recognising a supporting topos

First are the update rules for when the agent has a topos linking the two parts of the conditional: either in the direction with the antecedent as the parent in the link, or in the opposite direction with consequent as parent (though only if no topos with the default direction is known). The direction of antecedent as parent is 'default' in the sense that it should be preferred if distinct topoi in both directions are available, and is the direction assumed in case neither a supporting topos nor a conflicting one is found. The update in case of a supporting topos in the antecedent-consequent direction is given in (13):

[2] defined in (9) as Austinian propositions as per Ginzburg (2012)

(13) *default direction, ant→cons:*

$$\left[\begin{array}{ll} \text{pre}: & \left[\begin{array}{ll} \text{priv}: & \left[\begin{array}{ll} \text{Topoi} & : \{\text{Topos}\} \\ t & : \text{Topos} \\ c_{member} & : t \in \text{Topoi} \\ c_{def} & : \textit{enthMatch}(x : X, t) \end{array}\right] \\ \text{dgb}: & \left[\text{Moves}[0] = \text{Assert}(\text{if}(\text{a}, \text{b})) \quad : \text{LocProp}\right] \end{array}\right] \\ \text{effects}: & \left[\text{dgb}: \left[\begin{array}{l} \text{enths} = \text{pre.dgb.enths} \\ \qquad \cup\ \textit{enhanceEnth}(x : X, t) : \{\text{Enth}\} \\ \text{Topoi} = \text{pre.dgb.Topoi} \cup \text{pre.priv}.t : \{\text{Topos}\} \end{array}\right]\right] \end{array}\right]$$

where X is the type

$$\left[\begin{array}{l} \text{nodes} = \\ \quad \{\text{a.sit-type}_1, \text{b.sit-type}_2\} : RT_i \\ \text{links} = \\ \quad \{\langle \text{a.sit-type}_1, \text{b.sit-type}_2 \rangle\} : \langle RT_i, RT_i \rangle \\ \text{probs} = \\ \quad \{\text{P}(\text{b.sit-type}_2 \mid \text{r} : \text{a.sit-type}_1) = 0.95\} : \text{PI} \end{array}\right]$$

This rule may be applied following assertion of a conditional, where an agent knows a topos t that matches an enthymeme based on the content of the conditional, with a link from antecedent to consequent. In this case, the agent may add such an enthymeme enhanced with the topos to their *enths*, and add the underlying topos to the set of currently active topoi in the conversation.

Where such an option does not exist, a topos with only a link from consequent to antecedent can be used. The enthymeme added to *enths* in this case will contain a link only in the *ant←cons* direction. In practice, this means that any topoi supporting a link from antecedent to consequent take precedence over topoi which only reflect a link from consequent to antecedent. Relative to (13), the update rule for this case has constraints in its preconditions that (i) there are no topoi with a link in the *ant→cons* direction, but (ii) there is a known topos that supports an enthymeme in the alternative order. This topos is used to enhance such an enthymeme in *effects*.

The following is a simplified example using this second 'alternative order' rule for evidential conditionals. For space, members of *links* and *probs* are referenced by their index in *nodes* bolded.

(14) "If the glass fell, the cat pushed it."

a. Type of i : *InfoState*, a candidate for the second update rule

$$\left[\begin{array}{ll} \text{priv}: & \left[\text{Topoi} = \left\{\left[\begin{array}{l} \text{nodes} = \left\{\left[\begin{array}{l} x : \text{Ind} \\ y : \text{Ind} \\ \text{c}_{push} : \text{push}(x, y) \end{array}\right]_1, \left[\begin{array}{l} x = 1.y : \text{Ind} \\ \text{c}_{fall} : \text{fall}(x) \end{array}\right]_2\right\} \\ \text{links} = \langle \mathbf{1}, \mathbf{2} \rangle \\ \text{probs} = \{\text{P}(\mathbf{2} \mid r : \mathbf{1}) = 0.95\} \end{array}\right], \ldots\right\}\right] \\ \text{dgb}: & \left[\text{Moves}[0] = \text{Assert}\left(\text{if}\left(\left[\begin{array}{l} \text{sit} = \left[\begin{array}{l} x = \text{obj}_3 \\ \text{c}_{glass} = \text{glass}(\text{obj}_3) \\ \text{c}_{fall} = \text{fall}(\text{obj}_3) \end{array}\right] \\ \text{sit-type} = \left[\begin{array}{ll} x & : \text{Ind} \\ \text{c}_{glass} & : \text{glass}(x) \\ \text{c}_{fall} & : \text{fall}(x) \end{array}\right] \end{array}\right], \left[\begin{array}{l} \text{sit} = \left[\begin{array}{l} x = \text{obj}_4 \\ y = \text{obj}_3 \\ \text{c}_{cat} = \text{cat}(\text{obj}_4) \\ \text{c}_{push} = \text{push}(\text{obj}_4, \text{obj}_3) \end{array}\right] \\ \text{sit-type} = \left[\begin{array}{ll} x & : \text{Ind} \\ y & : \text{Ind} \\ \text{c}_{cat} & : \text{cat}(x) \\ \text{c}_{push} & : \text{push}(x, y) \end{array}\right] \end{array}\right]\right)\right)\right] \end{array}\right]$$

b. Type of i' : *InfoState*, the result of applying the update rule to i

$$\left[\text{dgb}: \left[\begin{array}{ll} \text{enths} = i.\text{dgb.enths} \cup \left[\begin{array}{l} \text{nodes} = \left\{\left[\begin{array}{l} x = \text{obj}_4 : \text{Ind} \\ y = \text{obj}_3 : \text{Ind} \\ \text{c}_{cat} : \text{cat}(x) \\ \text{c}_{push} : \text{push}(x, y) \end{array}\right]_1, \left[\begin{array}{l} x = \text{obj}_3 : \text{Ind} \\ \text{c}_{glass} : \text{glass}(x) \\ \text{c}_{fall} : \text{fall}(x) \end{array}\right]_2\right\} \\ \text{links} = \langle \mathbf{1}, \mathbf{2} \rangle \\ \text{probs} = \{\text{P}(\mathbf{2} \mid r : \mathbf{1}) = 0.95\} \end{array}\right] & : \{\text{Enth}\} \\ \text{Topoi} = i.\text{dgb.Topoi} \cup t & : \{\text{Topos}\} \end{array}\right]\right]$$

where t is the topos specified in *priv.Topoi* in (14a)

3.2.2 New information

Even without a guiding topos, conditionals allow us to express or learn information via an assumption that there is a positive connection between antecedent and consequent – provided we do not already know that the two are independent, or that the consequent shouldn't follow from the antecedent.

The last rule describes this case, where the agent's known topoi have neither evidence about a link between the antecedent or consequent, about the definite absence of one, or about a conflicting link. In this case, an 'enthymeme' with a link in the *ant→cons* direction may be added to *enths* solely on the basis of the conditional content. No additional topos is added to the list of active topoi – the process for generalising an acceptable enthymeme to a re-usable topos is not addressed here.

Recall that the topoi in an agent's resources may conflict with each other, and by necessity one of them was learned first: despite this, a conditional does not lead to formation of an acceptable enthymeme when such a clashing topos is already present. The shorthand for presence of a clashing topos is given in (15) as *enthClash*. An enthymeme clashes with a topos where the equivalent parent nodes lead to mutually exclusive child nodes, i.e. child nodes where a true type cannot be formed from their meet.

(15) *enthClash*(e : Enth, t : Topos) : Bool, **true** iff
$\exists x_i, y_j \in e.nodes, p_i, q_j \in b.nodes, x_i \sqsubseteq p_i$
$\exists \langle x'_i, y'_j \rangle \in e.links, x'_i \sqsubseteq x_i, y'_j \sqsubseteq y_j, \exists \langle p'_i, q'_j \rangle \in t.links, p'_i \sqsubseteq p_i, q'_j \sqsubseteq q_j,$
and $\neg T$, where $T = y'_j \wedge q'_j$

Relative to the previous two update rules, the preconditions in this rule specify that *priv.Topoi* has no topos supporting an enthymeme with a link between the antecedent and consequent in either direction, or a link which clashes with the possible conditional enthymeme, and also does not contain a topos supporting an enthymeme with an explicit constraint enforcing independence between the two.

4 Conclusion

The acceptability of a conditional is often determined by the conditional probability of the consequent on the antecedent, and recognition of some meaningful link between the two. However, both intuitively and according to experimental evidence, positive acceptability judgements can still be made without foreknowledge of such a connection. This paper presented two proposals on the basis that the knowledge enabling these judgements is topoic, integrating these factors into the representation of the dialogue state and agent resources. First, a formalisation of enthymemes and topoi as graphs was presented, on the grounds that they should be in the same form as other knowledge about causal and correlational relationships. Second, update rules for conditionals using topoi and enthymemes were presented, drawing on topoi to recognise the presence and direction of a 'meaningful' connection between antecedent and consequent, and making an assumption of one in the absence of any evidence.

There are several avenues for further work. Most work focuses on declarative conditionals, the most common form by far. However, conditional clauses are also used to form conditionalised questions and directives. The proposals here should be related to these forms, whether because to an extent they apply in those cases too, or because this topoic association is exclusive to declarative conditionals. This paper has also said nothing about more standard propositional aspects of conditionals. The proposals here about structural knowledge associated with conditionals should be integrated with this more standard fare.

Acknowledgements

Thanks to Jonathan Ginzburg for helpful discussion of and feedback on this work. This project has received funding from the European Union's Horizon 2020 research and innovation programme under the Marie Skłodowska-Curie grant agreement No 665850.

References

Bennett, J. (2003, April). A Philosophical Guide to Conditionals. Oxford University Press.

Breitholtz, E. (2014a). Enthymemes in Dialogue: A micro-rhetorical approach. Ph. D. thesis, University of Gothenburg.

Breitholtz, E. (2014b). Reasoning with topoi – towards a rhetorical approach to non-monotonicity. In Proceedings of the 50th anniversary convention of the AISB, 1st–4th April.

Breitholtz, E. (2015, August). Are widows always wicked? learning concepts through enthymematic reasoning. In R. Cooper and C. Retoré (Eds.), Proceedings of the TYTLES workshop on Type Theory and Lexical Semantics, Barcelona.

Breitholtz, E. and R. Cooper (2011). Enthymemes as rhetorical resources. In Proceedings of the 15th Workshop on the Semantics and Pragmatics of Dialogue (SemDial 2011), pp. 149–157.

Cooper, R. Type theory and language: From perception to linguistic communication. In prep.

Cooper, R. (2012). Type theory and semantics in flux. In R. Kempson, T. Fernando, and N. Asher (Eds.), Philosophy of Linguistics, Handbook of the Philosophy of Science, pp. 271 – 323. Amsterdam: North-Holland.

Cooper, R. and J. Ginzburg (2015). TTR for natural language semantics. In C. Fox and S. Lappin (Eds.), Handbook of Contemporary Semantic Theory (2 ed.)., pp. 375–407. Oxford: Blackwell.

Douven, I. (2008, September). The evidential support theory of conditionals. Synthese 164(1), 19–44.

Douven, I. and S. Verbrugge (2013, January). The probabilities of conditionals revisited. Cognitive Science 37(4), 711–730.

Edgington, D. (1995). On conditionals. Mind 104(414), 235–329.

Evans, J. S. B. T., S. J. Handley, and D. E. Over (2003). Conditionals and conditional probability. Journal of Experimental Psychology: Learning, Memory, and Cognition 29(2), 321–335.

Gillies, A. S. (2010). Iffiness. Semantics and Pragmatics 3, 1–42.

Ginzburg, J. (2012). The Interactive Stance. Oxford University Press.

Heim, I. (1982). The Semantics of Definite and Indefinite Noun Phrases. Ph. D. thesis, MIT.

Kratzer, A. (1986). Conditionals. Chicago Linguistics Society 22(2), 1–15.

Lewis, D. K. (1975). Adverbs of quantification. In E. L. Keenan (Ed.), Formal Semantics of Natural Language, pp. 3–15. Cambridge University Press.

Lewis, D. K. (1976, July). Probabilities of conditionals and conditional probabilities. The Philosophical Review 85(3), 297–315.

Oaksford, M. and N. Chater (2003, September). Conditional probability and the cognitive science of conditional reasoning. Mind and Language 18(4), 359–379.

Pijnacker, J., B. Geurts, M. van Lambalgen, C. C. Kan, J. K. Buitelaar, and P. Hagoort (2009, February). Defeasible reasoning in high-functioning adults with autism: Evidence for impaired exception-handling. Neuropsychologia 47(3), 644–651.

Skovgaard-Olsen, N., H. Singmann, and K. C. Klauer (2016, May). The relevance effect and conditionals. Cognition 150, 26–36.

Stalnaker, R. (1970, March). Probability and conditionals. Philosophy of Science 37(1), 64–80.

van Rooij, R. and K. Schulz (2019, March). Conditionals, causality and conditional probability. Journal of Logic, Language and Information 28(1), 55–71.

Author Index